Strategic READING 3
Building Effective Reading Skills

Teacher's Manual

CAMBRIDGE UNIVERSITY PRESS

Lynn Bonesteel

PUBLISHED BY THE PRESS SYNDICATE OF THE UNIVERSITY OF CAMBRIDGE
The Pitt Building, Trumpington Street, Cambridge, United Kingdom

CAMBRIDGE UNIVERSITY PRESS
The Edinburgh Building, Cambridge CB2 2RU, UK
40 West 20th Street, New York, NY 10011–4211, USA
10 Stamford Road, Oakleigh, VIC 3166, Australia
Ruiz de Alarcón 13, 28014 Madrid, Spain
Dock House, The Waterfront, Cape Town 8001, South Africa

http://www.cambridge.org

© Cambridge University Press 2004

It is normally necessary for written permission for copying to be obtained in advance from a publisher. The unit quizzes in this book can be copied and distributed in class. The normal requirements are waived here, and it is not necessary to write to Cambridge University Press for permission for an individual teacher to make copies for use within his or her own classroom. Only those pages which carry the wording "Copyright © Cambridge University Press" may be copied.

First published 2004

Printed in the United States of America

Typeface Adobe Caslon (Adobe®) System QuarkXPress® [AH]

A catalog record for this book is available from the British Library
Library of Congress Cataloging in Publication data available

ISBN 0 521 555809 Student's Book 1
ISBN 0 521 555779 Teacher's Manual 1
ISBN 0 521 555795 Student's Book 2
ISBN 0 521 555760 Teacher's Manual 2
ISBN 0 521 555787 Student's Book 3
ISBN 0 521 555752 Teacher's Manual 3

Illustrations:
Art direction, book design, and layout services: Adventure House, NYC

Contents

Introduction	v
Model lesson plan	ix
Teaching suggestions	1

UNIT 1	Superstitions	1
UNIT 2	Health	6
UNIT 3	Talent	11
UNIT 4	Beauty	16
UNIT 5	Technology	21
UNIT 6	Punishment	26
UNIT 7	Loss	30
UNIT 8	Memory	35
UNIT 9	Personality	40
UNIT 10	Celebrity	45
UNIT 11	The circus	50
UNIT 12	Martial arts	55

UNIT 13	Fashion	60
UNIT 14	The media	65
UNIT 15	Art	70
UNIT 16	Humor	75

| Unit quizzes | 79 |
| Unit quiz answers | 95 |

Introduction

Strategic Reading: Building Effective Reading Skills is a three-level series for young-adult and adult learners of English. As its title suggests, it is designed to develop useful reading, vocabulary-building, and critical thinking skills. Each level features adapted texts from a variety of authentic sources, including newspapers, magazines, books, and websites. The series encourages students to examine important topics in their lives as they build essential reading skills.

The third level in the series, *Strategic Reading 3*, is aimed at intermediate to high-intermediate students. It contains 16 units divided into three readings on popular themes such as movies, fear, communication, and the paranormal.

Every unit begins by introducing new vocabulary and asking questions related to the theme. Each reading ranges in length from 500 to 600 words and is accompanied by a full page of activities. Pre-reading activities interest students in the lesson topic, while reading exercises develop crucial skills and provide opportunities for discussion and writing. The wrap-up at the end of each unit recycles and expands key vocabulary into additional exercises and puzzles. Engaging extension activities serve as a valuable link to the world outside the classroom.

Each unit is designed to take five to six hours of class time, if all the activities are completed and the readings are assigned as class work. The units (and the readings within units) can either be taught in the order they appear or out of sequence. The readings and exercises, however, increase in difficulty throughout the book. The reading skills developed in these exercises are listed and indexed in the Scope and sequence on pages vi-ix of the Student's Book.

Student's Book organization

Preview

Every unit begins with a brief summary of each reading in the unit. These summaries are followed by questions for writing or discussion. The questions stimulate students' interest in the readings and allow them to share their knowledge about the topic. In addition, vocabulary from the readings appears on the preview page. As students discuss the preview questions, they should be encouraged to ask about unfamiliar vocabulary.

A separate vocabulary exercise familiarizes students with vocabulary related to the unit theme. Pre-teaching this vocabulary gives students a chance to relate the words to their lives and also helps them feel more comfortable as they begin to read. The new vocabulary words appear several times throughout the unit, providing students with more opportunities to learn their meanings and uses.

Before you read

Before each reading, students complete one of four types of pre-reading exercises: *Predicting, Relating to the topic, Thinking about personal experience,* or *Using previous knowledge.* These exercises prepare students to read and help them connect the topic of the reading to their own lives. Students mark statements that are true about themselves, identify information they expect to read, and write down what they expect to learn.

Reading

One *Scanning* or *Skimming* exercise accompanies every reading. Students learn to either scan or skim a text to look for specific information before reading the whole text. Other activities in this section ask students to confirm predictions from the "Before you read" section, compare their experiences with the author's experiences or identify the author's purpose, opinion, tone, or intended audience.

After you read

The varied exercises in this section provide practice in all aspects of a skill and accommodate different learning and teaching styles. Skills and activities in this section focus on:

- **Main ideas** Students choose the main idea of a reading or a paragraph or identify an author's opinion or point of view.

- **Details** Students show their understanding of details or distinguish between a main idea and a detail.

- **Guessing vocabulary from context** Students use contextual clues, recognize similarity in meaning between words, or recognize different forms of word families.

- **Text organization** Students show understanding of reference words or add sentences to a paragraph.

- **Restatement and inference** Students make inferences based on the text or distinguish between a restatement and an inference.

The final exercise, *Relating reading to personal experience,* asks three open-ended questions that are closely connected to the topic of the reading. It gives students an opportunity to share their thoughts, opinions, and experiences in writing or in discussions. It is also a chance to review and use vocabulary introduced in the unit.

Wrap-up

Every unit ends with a one-page wrap-up. In these exercises, students use vocabulary from the unit. Although some of this vocabulary appears in the readings, new terms may be introduced here.

The final exercise provides an opportunity for students to use the vocabulary they have learned in a meaningful context. Students work on a project, prepare a presentation, or participate in a discussion related to the unit theme. These activities involve designing and conducting surveys, researching and giving presentations, or interviewing classmates or native speakers of English.

Reading tips

Every unit features a reading tip designed to provide students with a useful language point illustrated in the reading. These tips correspond to the reading skills that students practice after reading.

Vocabulary

Students are sometimes instructed to find out the meaning of words or phrases. There are several ways that you can suggest students do this:

- Work together to help each other with unfamiliar vocabulary.
- Ask you (or a native speaker) to explain unfamiliar words.
- Look up the meanings of unfamiliar words in an English dictionary, such as the *Cambridge Dictionary of American English*.
- Use a bilingual dictionary or pocket translator to look up words that are hard to explain (for example, the names of animals or sports). In general, however, the use of bilingual dictionaries is not recommended.

Teacher's Manual organization

A Teacher's Manual is available for each level of *Strategic Reading*. Each Teacher's Manual contains:

- a model lesson plan,
- specific teaching suggestions for each unit in the Student's Book, including additional vocabulary definitions, cultural notes, and answers to exercises in the Student's Book,
- photocopiable unit quizzes, and
- answers to unit quizzes.

Teaching suggestions

Teaching suggestions for each unit offer specific ideas on how to present the material and additional vocabulary. Only vocabulary items that are not defined or represented pictorially in the Student's Book have been included. These items are defined as they are used in the reading. In addition, variations and optional activities have been provided to further expand upon reading topics, vocabulary, and exercises. Answers to the exercises in the Student's Book and some explanations have also been provided.

Unit quizzes

Photocopiable quizzes for each unit can be found at the back of this Teacher's Manual. Each quiz contains a 150- to 175-word reading related to the unit theme and a half-page of reading skills exercises. The quizzes measure general reading comprehension and ability to use basic reading strategies. Every quiz includes a *Guessing meaning from context* vocabulary exercise. Although individual vocabulary items are not tested separately, some of the unit vocabulary appears in each quiz reading. Suggested scores are included in the direction lines of all exercises. An answer key for all the quizzes can also be found at the back of the book.

Model lesson plan

Each unit of *Strategic Reading 3* can be divided into five lessons — one preview lesson, three lessons based on readings, and one wrap-up lesson. The entire unit should take approximately five to six hours to complete.

This lesson plan can serve as a generic outline to guide you through a lesson. It can be used with any unit of the Student's Book. For specific ideas on how the material can be presented or further expanded, refer to the Teaching suggestions for each unit.

Preview

The summaries, questions, and vocabulary on the preview page are intended to get the students interested in the readings and give them an opportunity to share their knowledge about reading topics.

Theme *(approximately 20-30 minutes)*

1. Give students a few minutes to read the preview questions. As students read, circulate and answer questions.

2. When students have read the questions, have them form pairs to discuss their answers. Tell them they will report at least one of their partner's answers to the class.

3. After 15–20 minutes, ask several students to share something their partners told them.

> *Variations:*
> - Assign step 1 as homework.
> - Assign step 2 as a small group discussion. Have each group report on something interesting from their discussion.
> - Ask students to answer the unit preview questions in writing, either at home or in class. Have them read their partner's responses in class and compare them to their own responses.

Vocabulary *(approximately 15-20 minutes)*

1. Tell students they will be learning new vocabulary that they need for the readings in the unit.

2. Choose a word from the vocabulary exercise. Write it on the board, and ask questions related to the word and the unit theme.

3. Have students complete the vocabulary exercise in pairs. Encourage them to use examples when they explain the meanings of words. Allow the use of dictionaries only if neither student knows the word.

4. After a few minutes, reassemble the class and help students with any words they still don't know.

> *Variation*:
> - Have students complete the vocabulary exercise as homework and discuss any unknown words in class.

Reading 1

Before you read *(approximately 10-15 minutes)*

This section prepares students to read and helps them connect the topic of the reading to their own lives.

1. Explain the meanings of any unfamiliar words in the title of the reading.

2. Tell students to work alone on the *Thinking about personal experience* exercise. If necessary, they can refer to the vocabulary exercise on the Preview page. Help them with any unfamiliar vocabulary.

3. After a few minutes, elicit their responses. Write the results on the board.

> *Variation*:
> - Assign step 2 as pair or group work.

Reading *(approximately 15-20 minutes)*

This section provides students with valuable practice in reading for general or specific information. Before beginning, make sure students understand the difference between reading a text and skimming or scanning it. Explain that *skimming* is a quick reading for general ideas. You do not read carefully; instead, you look at the title, subtitles, charts, pictures, and graphs to find out about the text. *Scanning* is also a quick reading, but here you look for information to answer a specific question, such as a number, name, word, or phrase.

1. Have students complete the *Skimming* or *Scanning* exercise. Tell students to raise their hands when they think they have the correct answers. After a minute or two, ask the students who raised their hands first and check the answers.

2. Give the class about five to seven minutes to read the entire article. Students who finish early should begin to read the article again. Slower readers should push themselves to finish the passage in the given time. Do not allow students to use dictionaries during the first reading. Instead, suggest that students focus on main ideas and ignore or guess unfamiliar vocabulary. Explain that they will have an opportunity to learn the unfamiliar words later.

> *Variation:*
> - Assign step 2 as homework. Make sure students understand that they should not use a dictionary.

After you read *(approximately 40-50 minutes)*

The purpose of these activities is to develop specific reading skills.

1. Tell students to work individually on the first exercise. Answer the first item together to make sure students understand the exercise. After a few minutes, have them compare their answers with a partner and discuss any differences. As they work, circulate and check their answers.

2. Have students complete the second exercise in pairs. Explain the purpose of the exercise (indicated in the Teaching suggestions), and answer the first item together.

3. When students finish, go over the exercise. Ask individual students to explain their answers.

4. Have students discuss the questions in *Relating reading to personal experience* in pairs. After about ten minutes, ask several students to share one of their answers.

> *Variations:*
> - Before the students begin a new reading, bring in something real (realia) connected to the topic, such as a photograph, poster, or musical recording. This will make the topic more meaningful. Some ideas for realia are provided in the Teaching suggestions.
> - *Relating reading to personal experience* questions can be answered in small groups, rather than in pairs.
> - *Relating reading to personal experience* questions can also be assigned as homework. Students can choose one question and respond to it in writing.

Follow the plan outlined above for the second and third readings in each unit. Try to vary the use of individual, pair, small group, and whole-class activities. You may choose to follow the same basic steps, but use some of the suggested variations to keep the lessons lively. To practice expressing their ideas in writing, students should write their answers to at least one of the *Predicting* and one of the *Relating reading to personal experience* exercises in each unit. Encourage students to use new vocabulary from the unit when they write. When possible, collect their work and return it to them with your comments.

Wrap-up *(approximately 60 minutes)*

The purpose of this page is to provide an opportunity for students to review and apply new vocabulary in a meaningful context.

1. Have students work alone on the Vocabulary expansion exercise(s). Use one item as an example to make sure that students understand the task. When students are finished, have them check their answers in pairs.

2. Follow the instructions for the final activity on the Wrap-up page. Although these activities usually involve student interaction, others are appropriate for individual or pair work.

3. Tell students that there will be a quiz on the unit based on their comprehension and reading skills, not on specific vocabulary. Point out that the reading passage in the quiz will contain some vocabulary from the unit.

> *Variations*:
> - Use the Vocabulary expansion exercise(s) as a competition. Divide the class into teams of three or four students each. Set a time limit to complete the activity. The team that finishes the activity first is the winner.
> - The Vocabulary expansion exercise(s) can also be assigned as homework.
> - After the students complete all the exercises on the Wrap-up page, a variety of games and activities can be used to review the unit vocabulary.

UNIT 1 Superstitions

PREVIEW
Page 1

Additional vocabulary

boogeyman: an imaginary monster that is used to frighten children
curse: a wish for something evil to happen (to someone or something)
evil eye: a look that some people believe has the magical power to injure or harm people
fortune: the good and bad events that happen to you
herb: a type of plant used in medicine
prognostication: a statement giving knowledge about the future
root: the part of a plant that grows down into the earth
tale: a story or report that is invented or difficult to believe

Additional activity

Bring in pictures of objects associated with superstitions. Write the word *superstition* on the board and explain what it means. Hold up the pictures and ask the students if they know any superstitions associated with them. Then give examples of popular superstitions in English-speaking countries. Some suggestions for pictures and some superstitions associated with them follow.

1. a black cat *(A black cat brings bad luck if it crosses your path.)*

2. a salt shaker *(If you spill salt, throw some over your left shoulder to prevent bad luck.)*

3. the number 13 *(The number 13 is bad luck.)*

4. two crossed fingers *(If you cross your index finger and your middle finger on one hand before you do something, it's good luck.)*

5. a four-leaf clover *(If you find a four-leaf clover, it's good luck.)*

6. an open umbrella *(It's bad luck to open an umbrella inside a house or building.)*

7. a ladder *(It's bad luck to walk under a ladder.)*

8. a broken mirror *(If you break a mirror, you will have seven years of bad luck.)*

READING 1 · Two worlds
Pages 2-3

This reading is from a memoir about a child's fascination with tales of superstition.

Additional vocabulary

accordingly: in a way that suits the situation
be torn between: having to make a choice between two possibilities
fig: the edible fruit of a tree that grows in warm places
mulberry tree: a tree with small, soft, purple fruit
the lines were so easy to draw: it was very easy to distinguish between things

STRATEGY: Encourage students to have specific questions in mind when they scan a text. This will help them find what they're looking for quickly without having to read the entire text.

Reading skill

Guessing meaning from context

Point out to students that when they guess meaning from context, it is often enough to get a general understanding of the meaning of a word. It is not necessary to be able to define the word exactly. Thinking in terms of general meaning, for example good vs. bad, weak vs. strong, or same vs. different, is often sufficient.

STRATEGY: Have students circle the words in the text that helped them to guess the meaning of the target words.

ANSWERS

Reading
3

After you read

A
1. attractive
2. is very unusual and surprising
3. interesting
4. want
5. think it's reasonable

B
1, 3, 4, 6

Unit 1 · Superstitions

READING 2 — Lucky hats and other fishing superstitions
Pages 4-5

This reading describes some common superstitions among fishermen.

Additional vocabulary

> **attractant:** a substance that makes insects, fish, or animals come near
> **bait:** food that fishermen use to catch fish
> **cast:** the act of throwing a fishing line into the water
> **Come to think of it:** Now that I think about it
> **downright:** extremely or very greatly
> **hook:** a curved device used to catch or hold things
> **somewhere down the line:** at some unspecified time in the (usually distant) future
> **speculation:** the act of forming opinions without having the necessary information or facts

Reading skill

Making inferences

Have students circle the place(s) in the text that led them to make an inference. This will help them see that an inference is not a blind guess, but rather a logical conclusion based on information contained in the text itself.

STRATEGY: Have students circle the places in the text on which they are basing their inferences.

Reading
Good luck: 4, 5
Bad luck: 1, 2, 3, 6

After you read

A
1. boarding a vessel
2. critters lurked
3. anglers
4. freebie
5. merit
6. disguise
7. school
8. precarious

B
Positive: 2, 3
Negative: 1, 6
Neutral: 4, 5

Unit 1 • Superstitions

Additional activity

Before the students read the article, have them work in groups to come up with a list of tips on how to succeed in fishing. Do not mention superstitions. If possible, put at least one person who fishes in each group. After a few minutes, ask the groups to share their lists. Write their tips on the board. After students finish the scanning exercise, have them identify any tips on the board that were in the reading.

READING 3 A superstition about new calendars
Pages 6-7

This reading describes some problems caused by one of the writer's childhood superstitions.

Additional vocabulary

> **air:** manner or appearance
> **aloofness:** unfriendliness and refusal to participate in things
> **avert:** turn away (your eyes)
> **black-eyed pea:** a type of small, edible bean
> **bribe:** give someone money to persuade him or her to do what you want
> **contortion:** the act of twisting or bending unnaturally into a different shape or form
> **incredulously:** in a way that shows you don't believe something
> **pick up:** learn informally
> **(someone's) share of:** a lot of
> **southern:** referring to the southern United States
> **threshold:** the entrance to a building or room
> **Try as I might:** Although I tried hard

Reading skill

Understanding details

When students complete true and false exercises, ask them to find and circle the details in the text that support their answers. This way, you can make sure that they understand the specific question, and are not simply scanning the text for familiar words.

STRATEGY: Encourage students to look for and underline details that help them decide if statements are true or false.

> **ANSWERS**
>
> **Reading**
> *Answers will vary.*
>
> **After you read**
>
> **A**
> 1. F (The children in the writer's family used to throw a quarter into a pot of black-eyed peas for good luck.)
> 2. F (People in the south of the United States thought that if a man were the first to enter the home on New Year's Day, the family would have good luck.)
> 3. F (The writer thought that if he waited until January to look at a new calendar, he wouldn't have bad luck.)
> 4. T
> 5. T
> 6. F (The actual superstition was not to hang a calendar before the New Year.)
>
> **B**
> a. 9
> b. 12

WRAP-UP
Page 8

> **ANSWERS**
>
> **A**
> *Positive in meaning:* 2, 5, 7, 8
> *Negative in meaning:* 1, 3, 4, 6, 9
>
> **B**
> 1. lost
> 2. some
> 3. ended
> 4. Too bad you lost.
> 5. it started to rain
> 6. always
> 7. got
> 8. am going to take
> 9. hard

Additional activity

Have students research an unfamiliar superstition and explain it to the class. Have them use a variety of sources for their research, including people from their own cultures, people from other cultures, the Internet, magazines, newspapers, and books.

UNIT 2 Health

PREVIEW
Page 9

Additional vocabulary

allergy: a condition that makes people very sensitive to something they eat, breathe, or touch

cataract: an area of the eye that changes to become unclear, causing poor eyesight

diabetes: a disease in which the body cannot control the amount of sugar in the blood

hacking cough: a loud cough that sounds painful

kidney stone: a mass of stone-like material that forms in the kidney and causes pain

life expectancy: the length of time that someone is expected to live

obesity: the condition of being extremely and unhealthily fat

Additional activity

Before students begin the vocabulary exercise, explain that more than one answer is possible in some cases. After they complete the exercise, write the three categories (Medication, Surgery, and Medication and Surgery) on the board. Call out each word or phrase from the box and ask students how they categorized it. When students disagree, have them defend their answers.

> **POSSIBLE ANSWERS**
> *Medication:* an allergy, an infection, a hacking cough, high blood pressure, diabetes
> *Surgery:* a cataract, a kidney stone
> *Medication and surgery:* cancer, heart disease, obesity

READING 1 Diets of the world
Pages 10-11

This reading explains why people from some countries suffer fewer diet-related illnesses.

Additional vocabulary

cod: a kind of lean, white fish
flaky: coming off easily in small, flat, thin pieces
flows freely: exists in large quantities
monounsaturated fatty acids: fat containing chemicals that people believe are healthy
not take something lightly: said or treated in a serious way
quintessentially: typically; usually
saturated fat: fat containing chemicals that people believe are unhealthy
savor: enjoy slowly, in order to appreciate it as much as possible
shavings: small, very thin pieces

Reading skill

Recognizing tone

Encourage students to think about a writer's tone when they read and highlight the parts of the text that clarify the writer's attitude or opinion.

It is often difficult for students to recognize the tone of a reading. To help them develop this skill, have them get in the habit of highlighting words, phrases, or sentences in a text that give clues to the writer's attitude or tone. For example, in this text they might highlight the research studies and statistics. This data and evidence of research suggests that the writer takes a thoughtful approach to diet-related illness.

STRATEGY: As they read, encourage students to highlight words, phrases, or sentences that indicate the writer's tone.

ANSWERS

Reading
1. French
2. Mediterranean
3. Chinese, Mediterranean
4. American
5. Chinese
6. Mediterranean
7. French
8. American

After you read

A
4

B
1. h   3. c   5. b   7. e
2. g   4. i   6. d   8. a

Unit 2 • Health

READING 2 — Drink, blink, and rest
Pages 12-13

This reading offers tips to help keep your eyes healthy.

Additional vocabulary

coming under strain: getting more stress or pressure
dehydrate: (cause to) lose water; dry
electro-magnetic: having magnetic and electrical parts
farsighted: unable to see nearby objects clearly
infrared: referring to light that cannot be seen but gives out heat
nearsighted: unable to see distant objects clearly
ozone layer: a layer of the atmosphere that stops harmful sunlight from reaching the earth
shield: protect
short-wave ultraviolet ray (UV ray): radiation waves that are shorter than visible light but longer than X-rays
susceptible to: easily harmed by

Reading skill

Distinguishing main ideas from details

Students often find it difficult to understand the difference between main ideas and details. After students complete exercise B, have them identify main ideas (M) and details (D). Remind students that the main ideas often (but not always) appear in the first sentence of a paragraph.

STRATEGY: Encourage students to underline main ideas and circle details in a text.

ANSWERS
Reading
All statements are true.

After you read
A
1, 3, 6

B
1. c   5. f
2. b   6. e
3. a   7. g
4. d

READING 3 — Azeri hills hold secret of long life
Pages 14-15

This reading reveals why an unusual number of people in Azerbaijan live to be over 100 years old.

Additional vocabulary

> **amid:** in the middle of
> **appreciably:** in a large enough way to be noticeable
> **barely give (something or someone) a second glance:** pay little or no attention to (something or someone)
> **cane:** a stick people lean on to help them walk
> **dismissively:** in a way that shows something or someone is not important and not worth considering
> **dry up:** disappear gradually
> **heartland:** the central or most important area
> **herd:** make animals move together as a group
> **longevity:** long life
> **predisposition:** likelihood to behave in a particular way
> **saffron:** the dried part of a flower used as a spice in cooking
> **shrug:** raise one's shoulders up and down to express a lack of knowledge

Reading skill

Guessing meaning from context

Encourage students to circle words that helped them guess the meaning of the target word or expression. Point out that often the words that help them are not in the same sentence, or even the same paragraph as the target word or expression. For example, the word *mountain* (par. 6) may help them guess the meaning of the word *slope* (par. 7).

STRATEGY: Encourage students to look for and circle context clues in sentences that precede or follow the sentence with the unfamiliar word.

ANSWERS

Reading
1, 3, 4, 6

After you read

A
1. the view
2. the mountains
3. Mr. Ibadov and his wife
4. Mr. Ibadov
5. Miri Ismailov's family
6. Mr. Ismailov and his great-great-grandson
7. herbs
8. life span

continued on next page

> **B**
> 1. e   2. d   3. a   4. b   5. f   6. g   7. c
>
> **C**
> 1. F (Amburdere is a region in the mountains of southern Azerbaijan.)
> 2. T
> 3. F (Mr. Ibadov can still do some kinds of work.)
> 4. F (Both Miri Ismailov and his great-great-grandson have never been to a doctor.)
> 5. F (Elmira Ismailov is not a doctor, but she uses herbs as medicines.)
> 6. T

Cultural notes

The Caucasus The Caucasus refers to a region located between the Black and Caspian Seas. It includes the Caucasus Mountains and surrounding lowlands. Independent nations in the area include Russia, Georgia, Armenia, and Azerbaijan.

Azerbaijan Azerbaijan is an independent nation on the southern slopes of the Caucasus Mountains. It was a republic of the Soviet Union until 1936, when it became an independent nation.

WRAP-UP
Page 16

> **ANSWERS**
>
> **A**
> 1. n   5. [C/U]
> 2. v   6. (fig.)
> 3. adj   7. [I]
> 4. [C]
>
> **B**
> 1. *Answers may vary.*
> a. people who limit their food and drink to lose weight
> b. trying to lose weight by eating less
> c. with less sugar or fat than usual
> d. trying to lose weight by eating less
> 2. Sentences a, c, and e are correct. Sentences b and d are incorrect.
>   b. *Diet* and exercise are important for good health.
>   d. They have been *dieting for* several weeks.

Additional activity

Have students search the Internet for surveys that use questions about lifestyle and genetic predisposition to estimate life expectancy. Choose one survey and have the students complete it. Discuss the results as a class.

UNIT 3 Talent

PREVIEW
Page 17

Additional vocabulary

burnout: extreme tiredness usually caused by working too much
Dame: a British title that goes in front of a woman's name
gifted: having great natural ability
prodigy: an unusually talented child
setback: a delay that prevents the progress of something or someone

Additional activity

After students complete the vocabulary exercise, review the meanings of the target vocabulary. Think of one famous person for each sentence and write their names on the board. Ask the students to match them with the sentences. When they finish, ask them to think of other famous people who fit the sentences. Write their names on the board.

READING 1 — A prodigy in mother's eyes
Pages 18-19

This reading describes the narrator's memory of a time her mother pushed her to become a prodigy.

Additional vocabulary

bay: an area of water surrounded by land on three sides
crazed: crazy; behaving wildly
drill: teach using repetition
foghorn: a warning device that makes a loud, low warning sound
Formica®: thin, hard plastic used to cover tabletops and other pieces of kitchen furniture

Reading skill

Guessing meaning from context

See the Teaching suggestions for this skill on page 2.

Additional activity

If possible, get a copy of the novel *The Joy Luck Club* by Amy Tan. After students complete exercises A, B, and C, read one or two pages that follow the excerpt aloud. (The excerpt comes from the chapter *Two Kinds*.) Then have students discuss the questions in exercise D.

ANSWERS
Reading
1, 2, 3, 4, 5, 6
After you read
A
2
B
1. e   2. d   3. c   4. b   5. a
C
2, 3, 4

Cultural notes

Ripley's Believe It or Not*, *Good Housekeeping*, and *Reader's Digest These are popular magazines in the United States and Canada. *Ripley's Believe It or Not* has true stories about extraordinary people and events. *Good Housekeeping* contains articles about home decorating, cooking, and family life. *Reader's Digest* has articles on topics of general social interest, including many articles about family life and extraordinary people or events.

Chinatown In the United States and Canada, Chinatown refers to a part of the city where many Chinese people live. This story takes place in San Francisco's Chinatown.

READING 2 Born to paint
Pages 20-21

This reading describes what life is like for a child who is also a very talented artist.

Additional vocabulary

acrylic: a type of paint
crayon: a stick of colored wax used for drawing
cubist: related to a modern art style that shows objects as sets of different geometric shapes
graduate: move from a lower to a higher level (of a skill or activity)
introverted: shy
oils: thick paints with an oil base

continued on next page

Omigosh: an exclamation used to express any strong emotion, especially surprise
scholastically: related to school and education
shake up: cause large changes to (something)
tight: limited in availability; scarce
unitary: limited to one; single
vignette: a short, descriptive piece of writing

Reading skill

Making inferences

Have students circle the place(s) in the text that led them to make an inference. This will help them see that an inference is not a blind guess, but rather a logical conclusion based on information contained in the text itself.

STRATEGY: Have students circle the places in the text on which they are basing their inferences.

ANSWERS

Reading
1, 2, 3, 5, 6

After you read

A
1. fascinated
2. surrender to
3. display early talent
4. notice
5. uses your energy

B
1. a
2. c
3. c

READING 3 — The sound of silence
Pages 22-23

This reading reveals why Dame Julie Andrews isn't singing anymore.

Additional vocabulary

gossip: a report (often cruel) about the behavior of another person; a rumor
grief therapy: psychological treatment that helps people deal with great sadness, such as death or loss
lyrics: words of a song

continued on next page

on hold: delayed
pending: while waiting for
polyp: a small group of diseased cells that grows in the body and is usually harmless
stock: routine
substantial: very large or important
sum (something) up: give a brief explanation of (something)
synonymous with: closely connected (in people's minds) so that one thing suggests the other
take (something or somewhere) by storm: be suddenly extremely successful
vocal cords: the part of the throat that produces sound

Additional activity

If possible, play a recording of Julie Andrews singing the theme song from *The Sound of Music* (or another song) before the students read the text. Elicit information about her (e.g., who she is, what movies she is in). Ask students to explain whether they like her voice, and give reasons.

Reading skill

Understanding main ideas

Explain that the main idea of a paragraph in English is usually contained in the first or last sentence of the paragraph. In interviews, they may be answers to the writer's questions. These answers are often set in quotation marks to indicate that they are the person's exact words. For example, in par. 7, "I think to some degree, I'm in a form of denial about it. . . ." answers the question "Do you think you're in denial about the future?"

STRATEGY: Encourage students to look for quotation marks to find answers to writers' questions.

ANSWERS

Reading
She had lost her ability to sing.

After you read

A
1. c   5. b
2. d   6. e
3. f   7. h
4. g   8. a

B
a. X   e. 9
b. 2   f. 6, 7
c. X   g. 4, 5
d. 6, 8

Page 24

> **ANSWERS**
> **A**
> 1. d 5. j
> 2. h 6. e
> 3. i 7. f
> 4. a 8. c
>
> **B**
> *Answers will vary.*

Additional activity

Have students research a child prodigy, either living or dead, and do a short presentation for the class. Some possibilities include Wolfgang Amadeus Mozart, Ludwig van Beethoven, Pablo Picasso, Bobby Fisher, Shirley Temple, Celine Dion, and Leonardo DaVinci.

UNIT 4 Beauty

PREVIEW
Page 25

Additional vocabulary

> **appeal:** attractiveness
> **beauty pageant:** a competition among people (usually women) based largely on their physical appearance
> **cosmetic surgery:** a medical operation that is used to improve someone's appearance
> **executive:** a person responsible for the decisions in a business
> **get ahead:** succeed
> **knockout:** a very attractive person
> **looks:** (someone's) physical appearance
> **undergo:** experience (something unpleasant)
> **vain:** too proud of one's appearance or achievements

Additional activity

Bring in magazine pictures of five attractive men and five attractive women. Hang them up with a number under each picture. Ask students to choose the man and woman they find most attractive. Tally the number of students who choose each picture in charts like this:

Pictures of Men

	Male Students	Female Students
Picture 1		
Picture 2		
Picture 3		
Picture 4		
Picture 5		

Pictures of Women

	Male Students	Female Students
Picture 1		
Picture 2		
Picture 3		
Picture 4		
Picture 5		

Discuss any patterns that emerge.

READING 1 — Executives go under the knife
Pages 26-27

This reading explains how cosmetic surgery is helping some executives to succeed.

Additional vocabulary

catch on to: notice
irrelevance: not having importance
promotion: an advancement to a more important position in a company
recruitment consultant: a person whose job is to find new employees for companies
self-esteem: respect for oneself
sub-surgical procedure: a medical procedure that is not too serious
trend: the general direction of changes or developments
wrinkle: a small line in the skin, often as the result of aging

Reading skill

Guessing meaning from context

See the Teaching suggestion for this skill on page 2.

ANSWERS

Reading
1. Executive B
2. Executive A
3. Executive A
4. Neither executive

After you read

A
1. going under the knife
2. climb the career ladder
3. glass ceiling
4. passed over
5. prospects
6. preserve
7. bags

B
1. men and women
2. Men and women
3. women
4. women
5. Men
6. men

READING 2 What makes a man attractive?
Pages 28-29

This reading presents the results of a recent survey on what makes a man attractive.

Additional vocabulary

cavemen: people who lived in caves long before recorded history
feminized: having a female appearance
instinctively: naturally, without having to think
protruding: sticking out; pushing forward
provoke: cause
robust: strong and healthy
species: a group of animals or plants with common characteristics
testosterone: a male hormone that causes growth and change in older boys

Reading skill

Understanding reference words

Students often misunderstand a text if they misidentify the words that the related pronouns refer to. Point out that the pronouns *it*, *they*, and *them*, as well as the determiners *this*, *that*, *these*, and *those* can refer not only to nouns, but also to entire ideas.

STRATEGY: Encourage students to circle the pronouns and determiners in a text and to identify the nouns or ideas that they refer to.

Additional activity

To make sure students understand the vocabulary in this reading, have them label the photos on page 28 with the expressions from Before You Read. For example, have them label the relevant parts of Arnold Schwarzenegger's photo with *thick eyebrows*, *deep-set eyes*, *large jaw*, and *protruding forehead*.

> **ANSWERS**
> **After you read**
> **A**
> 1. beauty   4. men
> 2. face   5. men
> 3. perception of beauty   6. women
> **B**
> a. 2, 3   d. 1
> b. not in the text   e. not in the text
> c. 8, 9   f. 4, 5, 6, 7
>
> continued on next page

> **C**
> Researchers in *Scotland* interviewed men and women in *three* countries. They found that *women* prefer feminine male faces, but *men* prefer masculine male faces. Psychologist David Perrett is *surprised* about the findings. He says people associated *feminine* faces with emotional warmth, faithfulness, and cooperation; however, they associate *masculine* faces with coldness, dishonesty, and dominance. According to Perrett, years ago men chose women who seemed likely to *bear healthy children,* while women chose men for *more* complicated reasons. This study was published in a *journal* called Nature.

READING 3 — In the land of the mirror
Pages 30-31

This reading looks at the importance of beauty pageants in Venezuela.

Additional vocabulary

> **derive:** obtain or get
> **dermatologist:** a doctor who treats skin problems
> **dietitian:** a person who specializes in nutrition
> **get (someone) down:** cause (someone) to feel unhappy or depressed
> **gummy smile:** a smile that shows not only the teeth, but also the gums above the teeth
> **melting pot:** an environment where many cultures and races are mixed
> **nose job:** cosmetic surgery to improve the appearance of the nose
> **personal trainer:** a person who gives private fitness classes
> **put a lot into (something):** devoted much time and energy toward (something)
> **regimen:** a regulated system of diet and exercise used to improve fitness or health
> **rough diamond:** a person without experience or refinement who has the potential to be great
> **ticket to the good life:** opportunity to make a lot of money

Reading skill

Recognizing purpose

Before students begin the exercise, be sure they understand the meanings of *inform* (to give someone new information), *persuade* (to change someone's ideas, feelings, or actions), *entertain* (to amuse someone), and *inspire* (to make someone feel that they can do something). As they read, have them think about how the text affects them.

STRATEGY: Encourage students to think about how a text affects them.

> **ANSWERS**
>
> **Reading**
> 1, 3, 4, 6
>
> **After you read**
> **A**
> 1. a   4. e
> 2. c   5. g
> 3. h   6. d
>
> **B**
> 1

WRAP-UP
Page 32

> **ANSWERS**
>
> **A**
> *Referring only to men:* handsome, rugged
> *Referring only to women:* beautiful, lovely, pretty, stunning
> *Referring to men and women:* attractive, cute, elegant, good-looking, gorgeous, striking
>
> **B**
> *Answers will vary.*

Additional activity

Here is a way that students can perform their own beauty perception studies:

1. Divide the students into groups of three or four.
2. Have each group come up with a theory about beauty perception. For example:
   a. *Most people find large eyes more attractive than small eyes.*
   b. *Most men prefer women with long hair.*
   c. *Most women prefer tall men to short men.*
3. Have each group design an experiment using magazine pictures to test the theory.
4. Have each group test the theory on ten participants.
5. Have each group present its theory and findings to the class.

UNIT 5 Technology

PREVIEW
Page 33

Additional vocabulary

> **cyberspace:** the Internet
> **download:** copy or move (programs or information) into a computer's memory
> **joystick:** a movable handheld stick that controls the action of some computer games
> **keystroke:** the act of pressing down a key on a computer

Additional activity

Divide the class into groups of three or four students. Write this question on the board:

How do people use computer technology in their everyday lives?

Give the groups ten minutes to brainstorm as many ideas as possible. Then have them read their lists aloud. The group with the longest list wins.

READING 1 The car that thinks it's your friend
Pages 34-35

This reading describes a car of the future with some surprising features.

Additional vocabulary

> **drowsiness:** tiredness
> **emulate:** copy; imitate
> **glower:** looks angry or threatening
> **hood:** the metal cover over the engine of a car
> **lose your cool:** become angry or excited
> **menacing:** threatening to seriously harm someone or something
> **panel:** a flat rectangular part that fits into something larger
> **prick up:** suddenly stand up (like an animal's ears)
> **road rage:** a driver's uncontrolled anger, especially at another driver's behavior
> **sensor:** a device that receives a signal and responds to it
> **swerve:** suddenly change direction
> **touchy-feely:** openly expressing love and affection

Reading skill

Guessing meaning from context

See the Teaching suggestions for this skill on page 2.

> **ANSWERS**
> **Reading**
> 1, 4
> **After you read**
> **A**
> 1. headlights, hood, trunk
> 2. sits up, wags . . . tail
> 3. drowsiness, lose . . . cool
> **B**
> 1, 4, 7

Cultural note

Blade Runner *Blade Runner* was a science-fiction movie from 1982 that depicted life in 2020. In the movie, the police rode in spinners, menacing-looking vehicles that they could drive or fly.

READING 2 Identification, please!
Pages 36–37

This reading describes the latest technology used to verify people's identities.

Additional vocabulary

> **embedded:** placed firmly (in something)
> **employ:** use
> **exploding:** growing rapidly
> **implement:** put (a plan or system) into operation
> **iris:** the colored, circular part of an eye
> **plummet:** fall very quickly and suddenly

Reading skill

Understanding details

See the Teaching suggestions for this skill on page 4.

Additional activity

After students complete the reading, put them in groups of three or four. Have them discuss the different types of biometrics technologies presented in the reading. Encourage them to discuss any other biometrics technologies that they may be familiar with from movies or TV shows. Then have them rank the effectiveness of the different biometrics technologies.

22 Unit 5 • Technology

> **ANSWERS**
>
> **Reading**
> *Answers will vary.*
>
> **After you read**
>
> **A**
> 3
>
> **B**
> 1. ?
> 2. F (Biometrics technology is in use in many places already, including some airports, hospitals, prisons, and government buildings.)
> 3. T
> 4. T
> 5. F (Fingerprint scans compare a print scan to a stored file, while handprint scans measure a hand's unique geometric aspects.)
> 6. F (Currently, iris scans are the most accurate.)
> 7. T
> 8. ?
> 9. T

READING 3 — Researchers worry as teens grow up online
Pages 38-39

This reading describes some problems that result when teenagers spend a lot of time online.

Additional vocabulary

> **big fuss:** needless worry
> **catch-up time:** time to do something that you have not had time to do in the past
> **code:** a system of words, letters, or signs that represent a message in secret or short form
> **hang around with (someone):** spend a lot of time with someone
> **hangout:** a place where someone spends a lot of time
> **It's on so many people's minds:** Many people think about it.
> **leap at the chance:** be very eager (to do something)
> **mere:** unimportant
> **wired world:** the Internet and other modern communications technology

Reading skill

Restating and making inferences

It is not always easy for students to recognize restatements and to make inferences. When students practice these skills, have them find relevant parts of the text, that is, sentences or phrases that have the same meaning or lead to the inference. For example, for item 1 (*Spending a lot of time online affects teenagers' ability to form relationships*), relevant sentences or phrases are in paragraph two (. . . *as cyberspace replaces the pizza parlor, . . . adolescents are becoming more isolated . . .*) and paragraph four (*increased signs of loneliness and social isolation . . . fewer friends . . .*).

STRATEGY: Whenever students practice recognizing restatements or making inferences, have them highlight the relevant parts of the text.

ANSWERS

Reading
3

After you read

A
1. c 5. g
2. e 6. b
3. d 7. f
4. a

B
1. R 5. T
2. R 6. T
3. T 7. T
4. R 8. R

WRAP-UP
Page 40

ANSWERS

A
1. i   6. l
2. b   7. h
3. k   8. d
4. e   9. j
5. f   10. c

B

Answers may vary.
1. parent over shoulder
2. want to
3. before
4. Are you OK?
5. tomorrow
6. great
7. boyfriend/girlfriend
8. today

Additional activity

The topic of this reading is suitable for a class debate. Divide students into three teams: one in favor of teenagers using the Internet, one against, and one team of judges. Make sure that the groups are sitting far enough apart so that they cannot hear each other. Tell the opposing teams to make a list of arguments that support their position, and then think of ways the opposing team will argue against them. They should also make a list of questions to ask the opposing team. Meanwhile, the team of judges should make a list of arguments that they expect to hear from both sides, and develop a list of questions to ask the teams. Before the debate, make sure the students understand the rules, which will vary depending on class size, teacher preference, and class time. Here is a suggested set of rules:

1. Each team gets two minutes to make an opening statement. The order of the statements is determined by a coin toss.

2. The teams take turns asking questions for a set period of time (for example, 20 minutes in total, 10 minutes each). The judges keep time, making sure that both teams ask an equal number of questions, and speak for an equal amount of time.

3. The judges ask questions of both teams for a set period of time (for example, 10 minutes in total, five minutes for each team).

4. Each team gets one minute to make a final statement. The order of the statements is determined by a coin toss.

5. The judges meet and decide on a winner.

6. The judges announce the winner, giving specific reasons for their decision.

UNIT 6 Punishment

PREVIEW
Page 41

Additional vocabulary

act up: behave badly
inflict: force someone to experience something unpleasant
insolent: intentionally and rudely showing no respect
spank: hit on the bottom with the hand as a punishment
suspension: a punishment of temporarily not being allowed to go to school
take the fun out of (something): make (something fun) unpleasant
wrestle: fight with someone by holding him or her and trying to throw him or her to the ground

Additional activity

After the students have completed the vocabulary exercise, have them discuss their answers in groups. Encourage them to provide details or reasons for their answers.

READING 1 Spanking on trial
Pages 42-43

This reading reports on an American who was arrested in Canada for spanking his daughter.

Additional vocabulary

add fuel to (something): make (something that is causing conflict) even worse
at the heart of (something): the most important part of (something)
bring (something) into sharp focus: cause (an issue or idea) to be seen and understood more clearly
fetch: get and bring back
go over the line: behave inappropriately
hard feelings: bad thoughts or feelings (between two people or groups)
headache: something that causes anxiety
rage: continue strongly
so to speak: in a manner of speaking
step in (something): accidentally get involved in (something unpleasant)
testimony: spoken or written statement that something is true, especially into a court of law
verdict: the decision of a judge or jury

Reading skill

Understanding text organization

To understand how a text is organized, it's important to identify the main ideas of key paragraphs. Students can do this by summarizing the most important information in key paragraphs. For example, par. 1 can be summarized as follows: *A woman in Canada called the police when she saw an American man spank his daughter.*

STRATEGY: Encourage students to summarize the main ideas of key paragraphs on their own or in groups.

> **ANSWERS**
> **Reading**
> 1, 2, 3, 4
> **After you read**
> **A**
> 3
> **B**
> 1. b   3. a   5. d   7. c
> 2. f   4. g   6. e
> **C**
> a. 4   c. 1   e. 6
> b. 3   d. 3   f. 2

READING 2 — The letter
Pages 44–45

This reading tells the story of a girl who gets into trouble with her mother for receiving a letter.

Additional vocabulary

> **aimlessly:** without any clear intention, purpose, or direction
> **betrayal:** an act of disloyalty
> **dangle:** hang loosely
> **deceit:** an act of keeping the truth hidden, especially to get an advantage
> **demeanor:** a way of looking and behaving
> **hut:** a small, simple building
> **notion:** belief or idea
> **spit:** say quickly and angrily
> **sternly:** in a way that shows disapproval
> **stoic:** not showing any sign of the emotion
> **take hold of (someone):** take control of (someone)
> **wearily:** in a very tired manner

Reading skill

Understanding reference words

See the Teaching suggestions for this skill on page 18.

> **ANSWERS**
> **Reading**
> *Answers will vary.*
> **After you read**
> **A**
> 2
>
> **B**
> 1. H   3. F   5. F   7. F
> 2. F   4. H   6. H   8. F
>
> **C**
> *Possible answers:*
> 1. Hatsue is probably around 16 or 17 years old. (The writer refers to her as a *girl*, and her mother treats her like a child. However, the letter is from a boy who's in love with her.)
> 2. It's probably winter. (The writer mentions that Hatsue's face is "reddened by the cold" and she's wearing a scarf. Also, Fujiko "went out into the wind.")
> 3. He probably told Hatsue that he loved her.
> 4. She is probably a strong, serious, traditional woman. She is very strict with her daughter and expects her to obey her. She does not like to show her emotions.
> 5. She is generally an obedient daughter, and she feels guilty about deceiving her mother. She is less traditional than her mother and more likely to show her emotions.

READING 3   Schools take the fun out of suspension

Pages 46-47

This reading describes how suspension is changing in some California schools.

Additional vocabulary

> **all the sweeter:** even better
> **boost:** improve or increase
> **couldn't care less:** don't care at all
> **fall behind:** fail to do (something) fast enough or on time
> **have second thoughts:** reconsider a decision or action
> **in return:** in exchange
> **kick (someone) out:** force someone to leave, especially because of bad performance or behavior
> **snowball effect:** a situation that is somewhat bad quickly becomes much worse
> **study hall:** a period of time during the school day that is set aside for study
> **turn one's life around:** change one's life so it improves a lot
> **underlying:** existing, but not obvious or clear

Reading skill

Recognizing purpose

See the Teaching suggestions for this skill on page 19.

> **ANSWERS**
>
> **Reading**
> 2, 3, 4
>
> **After you read**
>
> **A**
> 2
>
> **B**
> 1. c   5. d
> 2. f   6. g
> 3. a   7. b
> 4. e

WRAP-UP
Page 48

> **ANSWERS**
>
> **A**
> *Possible answers:*
>
> | Adjective | Noun | Verb |
> |---|---|---|
> | 1. confrontational | confrontation | confront |
> | 2. deceitful | deceit | deceive |
> | 3. disciplinary | discipline | discipline or disciplined |
> | 4. effective | effect | affect |
> | 5. excessive | excess | exceed |
> | 6. penal | penalty | penalize |
> | 7. punishable or punitive | punishment | punish |
> | 8. suspended | suspension | suspend |
>
> **B**
> 1. punishable (adj)   5. deceive (v)
> 2. suspend (v)   6. exceed (v)
> 3. penalty, punishment (n)   7. confronted, punished, disciplined (v)
> 4. disciplinary, punitive (adj) 8. effect (n)

Additional activity

Before students begin exercise A, review the suffixes needed to change parts of speech:

1. To form adjectives, add *-al, -ive, -able, -ary, -ful,* or *-ed.*

2. To form nouns, add *-tion, -ty, -ment, -ion,* or no suffix.

3. To form verbs, add *-ize* or no suffix.

UNIT 7 Loss

PREVIEW
Page 49

Additional vocabulary

coffin: box in which a dead person is buried
condolence: an expression of sympathy with another's loss
funeral: a ceremony at which a dead person is buried or burned
grieve: feel great sadness, especially at the death of someone
hearse: a vehicle for carrying a coffin to a funeral
late: no longer alive, especially having recently died
mourning: feeling and expressing sadness about someone's death
procession: a line of people moving in the same direction in a formal way, especially as part of a ceremony

Additional activity

This unit deals with a subject that may be sensitive for students. It may be advisable to focus discussions on the cultural aspects of death rather than personal experiences. Here are additional discussion questions that can be used to introduce the topic:

1. At what age do you think children should be taught about death?
2. Do you think it's appropriate for children to attend a funeral ceremony?
3. How do people from your culture mark someone's death?

READING 1 Death and superstition
Pages 50-51

This reading describes some traditions and superstitions about death among people living in parts of the United States.

Additional vocabulary

court: date; pursue someone with the intent to marry
dictate: determined; decided
hang over (someone's) head: restricting or threatening (someone)
hymn: a song of praise, especially to God

continued on next page

> **I would dare say:** I think it's true that
> **preacher:** a person who gives religious speeches
> **sleek:** smooth and shiny, and therefore looking healthy and attractive
> **the hereafter:** life after death
> **wind its way:** follow a route that bends repeatedly in different directions

Reading skill

Recognizing similarity in meaning

Point out that many writers try to avoid repeating a word in a text. As a result, many texts contain synonyms or words with similar meanings. Teach students to expand their vocabularies by looking for synonyms of unfamiliar words in the same sentence or paragraph. Exercise A demonstrates the use of words with synonymous meanings within a single text.

STRATEGY: Encourage students to look at the text carefully when they find an unknown word. The surrounding sentences may contain a synonym that is more familiar.

ANSWERS

Reading
The picture was taken in the state of Kentucky, in a region of the United States called Appalachia.

After you read

A
1. d	3. f	5. c	7. h	9. j
2. a	4. e	6. g	8. i	10. b

B
Good luck: 4, 6
Bad luck: 1, 2, 3, 5, 7

Cultural notes

Appalachia and Kentucky The Appalachian Mountains extend for almost two thousand miles (3,200 kilometers) from the Canadian province of Newfoundland to central Alabama in the United States. Parts of the state of Kentucky are located in the Southern Appalachians, where, due to the isolation of mountain life, the people developed a distinctive culture with its own traditions and superstitions.

The American South The American (U.S.) South refers to the states of Alabama, Arkansas, Florida, Georgia, Kentucky, Louisiana, Maryland, Mississippi, North Carolina, Oklahoma, South Carolina, Tennessee, Texas, Virginia, and West Virginia. The American South has many unique traditions and superstitions that vary depending on the state or region.

READING 2 — Chapter Two
Pages 52-53

This reading is a scene from a play about how one man deals with the loss of his wife.

Additional vocabulary

> **bouncing:** walking in an energetic way
> **critic:** a person who reviews plays, movies, books, or art
> **defrost:** make (something) no longer frozen
> **flat:** (in British or Australian English) apartment
> **how dare (someone):** I'm very angry at (someone) for doing something
> **live out one's life:** live (in a particular way) until one dies
> **playwright:** a person who writes plays

Reading skill

Making inferences

See the Teaching suggestion for this skill on page 3.

Additional activity

Bring in some sympathy cards written in English. Pass them around the class and elicit any unfamiliar words or expressions. Write them on the board and explain them.

ANSWERS
Reading
1. He kept looking for his wife in all the places that they had been to together.
2. He finds a letter of condolence from someone who knew his wife.

After you read
A
1. a   2. c   3. b   4. c   5. b   6. b

B
1, 4, 5

Cultural note

King's Road and *Portobello* and *Harrods* *King's Road* and *Portobello* are popular shopping districts in London, England. *Harrods* is a famous London department store.

READING 3 — *Funeral Blues* and *The Chariot*
Pages 54-55

These readings are poems about the end of life.

Additional vocabulary

> **crepe:** soft, thin, light fabric
> **dismantle:** take (something) apart
> **mound:** a pile of earth or stones
> **scribble:** write or draw quickly and carelessly
> **'tis:** an old-fashioned, literary form of *It is*, often used in poems

Reading skill

Rhyming

Read the poems aloud. As students listen, have them underline the words that rhyme. Elicit which words are not exact rhymes (*telephones / bone* in "Funeral Blues"; *away / civility* and *day / eternity* in "The Chariot"). Have them complete exercise C.

ANSWERS

Reading
Answers will vary.

After you read

A
1. muffled
2. moaning
3. doves
4. immortality
5. haste
6. civility
7. cornice
8. surmised

B
1. b   2. a   3. b   4. a   5. a

C
1. bone
2. come
3. dead
4. gloves
5. rest
6. wrong
7. sun
8. good
9. Immortality
10. sun
11. mound
12. eternity

Cultural note

Nineteenth-century pronunciation The pronunciation of some sounds and words has changed since the nineteenth century. For example, in the nineteenth century the final vowel sounds of the words *civility* and *away* rhymed.

WRAP-UP
Page 56

> **ANSWERS**
> **A**
> 1. l   3. k   5. f   7. e   9. j   11. g
> 2. d   4. b   6. i   8. h   10. a   12. c
>
> **B**
> 1. twins   5. fives   9. fears
> 2. minds   6. gives   10. wears
> 3. love   7. knows   11. need
> 4. stove   8. cows   12. red

Additional activity

Have students find poems they like. Have them identify any words that rhyme and practice reading the poems aloud. Then have them read the poems aloud for the class.

UNIT 8 Memory

PREVIEW
Page 57

Additional vocabulary

diminish: decrease or be decreased in size or importance
eyewitness: a person who saw a crime or accident happen
lapse: a temporary failure

Additional activity

Tell students they have one minute to memorize the italicized words in the Vocabulary exercise. After one minute, have them close their books and write down all the words they remember. Then have them open their books and check their answers.

READING 1 Can you believe what you see?
Pages 58-59

This reading presents research on the reliability of memory.

Additional vocabulary

accomplice: a person who helps someone commit a crime
culprit: someone who has done something wrong
custody: the state of being confined, usually by the police
fleeting: brief or quick
from scratch: from the beginning
junction: the place where two or more things meet
leading question: a question that, because of the words in it, suggests the answer the questioner wants
loiter: stand or wait in a public place without doing anything
on one's own: alone, without any help
plant (something or someone): put (something or someone) in a position secretly, especially to deceive someone
sway: persuade

Reading skill

Distinguishing main and supporting ideas

Students often have difficulty distinguishing main and supporting ideas. Explain that main ideas tend to be more general, while supporting ideas tend to be more specific. For example, in exercise A, *Witnesses adapt their memories to include new information* is a general statement, and *Psychologists have studied eyewitness testimony* is a specific statement that supports this statement.

Additional activity

Have students do as much of exercise B as possible from memory. Compare answers as a class. Then, have students look back at the text to complete the chart and correct their answers. Encourage students to underline or highlight the phrases and sentences in the text that helped them complete the chart.

ANSWERS

Reading
1, 2, 3

After you read

A
1 a. M	2 a. S	3 a. S
b. S	b. M	b. M

B
1. 40
2. 39
3. Pairs were asked to decide whether the woman had an accomplice.
4. Each person saw a different picture.
5. 7
6. 8
7. Eyewitness testimony is not reliable.

READING 2 — Man weds the wife he forgot
Pages 60-61

This reading describes how complete memory loss affected one man and his family.

Additional vocabulary

> **all over again:** again
> **catastrophic:** suddenly causing very great trouble or destruction
> **claw back:** obtain possession of (something) again with difficulty

Additional activity

Divide the class into groups of three or four. Have each group do the predicting exercise together. Then, have group members write a short paragraph based on their prediction. Have the groups read their paragraphs aloud before they read the text.

Reading skill

Guessing meaning from context

See the Teaching suggestions for this skill on page 2.

ANSWERS

Reading

2

After you read

A

1. b   2. d   3. a   4. d

B

1. He had a heavy cold and severe headaches, went to the hospital, slipped into a coma, and was diagnosed with brain cancer. He came out of the coma with memory loss.
2. Things about modern life that surprised him included the cars people drive, the cost of everything, the way houses are, the way people dress and speak, music, color TV, video players, and CDs.
3. He could not remember the Kennedy assassination, the Beatles, Elvis Presley's death, or man walking on the moon.
4. He could not remember his wife or his children.
5. He could not remember meeting his wife, getting married, or having children.

Cultural notes

Kennedy assassination, the Beatles, Elvis Presley, **and** ***Man's first walk on the moon*** These cultural references are all associated with the United States during the 1950s and 1960s.

Kennedy assassination In 1963, the thirty-fifth president of the United States, John F. Kennedy, was assassinated in Dallas, Texas at the age of 46.

The Beatles Originally from Liverpool, England, *The Beatles* came to the United States in 1964 and became one of the most successful rock and roll bands in history.

Elvis Presley American popular singer Elvis Presley is considered the "King of Rock and Roll." He was one of the most successful performers from the mid-1950s until his death in 1977.

Man's first walk on the moon On July 20, 1969, Apollo 11 astronauts Neil Armstrong and Edwin Aldrin became the first human beings to walk on the moon. This event was televised and watched by people all over the world.

READING 3 — Repeat after me: Memory takes practice
Pages 62-63

This reading describes ways you can improve your memory.

Additional vocabulary

chiefly: mostly
embedded: fixed firmly into (something)
framework: an organized structure of ideas
given the fact that: since; because
in a sense: in some ways
inherently: existing naturally, in a way that is a natural or basic part of something, not able to be removed or changed
long division: the mathematical process of division in which the steps are indicated in detail
take a lot of headshots: repeatedly attempt to put a soccer ball into a net by using the head

Reading skill

Understanding reference words

See the Teaching suggestions for this skill on page 18.

ANSWERS

Reading
1. F (People of all ages worry about memory loss.)
2. T
3. T
4. F (The more time students spend on a subject, the better they remember it.)
5. F (There is no proof that having a better memory makes you smarter.)

After you read

A
1. Meghan Pierce
2. improved memory
3. Yo-Yo Ma's cello
4. an important date
5. the foundation
6. World War II

B
1. overload   2. keys   3. renowned   4. recovered   5. flawlessly

C
1. M; infrequency of use, new and different information, isolated facts
2. S; many things on students' minds
3. M; stress, physical trauma, limited brain capacity
4. S; Yo-Yo Ma left his cello in a New York City taxi.
5. M; lots of practice and better organization
6. S; keep things in same place every day, use word associations, mentally repeat things

WRAP-UP
Page 64

> **ANSWERS**
>
> **A**
> *Remember something well:* remember . . . as if it were yesterday; is fresh in my mind
> *Make someone remember something:* refresh my memory, jog your memory
> *Try hard to remember something:* is on the tip of my tongue, rack my brain
> *Remember something vaguely:* rings a bell
> *Have a bad memory:* been absent-minded, have a memory like a sieve, is . . . scatter-brained
>
> **B**
> *Answers will vary.*

Additional activity

Here is a fun memory game that students can use to review vocabulary from the unit.

1. Make a set of 20 large cards (large enough to be posted on the board and seen by all the students). Ten of the cards should have a vocabulary item written on one side, and the other ten should have the corresponding definitions of the ten items (one for each card).

2. Shuffle the cards well and place them face down on the board in a pattern of five rows and four columns. When they are on the board in a regular pattern, number them from 1 to 20 (i.e., first row 1–4, second row 5–8, and so on).

3. Divide the class into teams of no more than four students each.

4. Ask a student from Team A to call out two numbers at random. Turn over the cards that the student has chosen, and give the students time to read what is on the cards. If the two cards match, and Team A recognizes that they match, remove the two cards from the board and give them to Team A. Then, give Team A another turn. Proceed in the same fashion until Team A turns over two nonmatching cards. Then it is Team B's turn. Continue playing until all the cards are gone from the board. The team with the most cards wins.

UNIT 9 Personality

PREVIEW
Page 65

Additional vocabulary

boisterous: noisy, energetic, and undisciplined
conscientious: putting a lot of care and effort into one's work
extroverted: not shy; comfortable talking to others
inhibited: shy; not comfortable talking to others
predisposition: tendency to behave in a particular way
sullen: silent and unpleasant
withdrawn: preferring to be alone and not interested in others

Additional activity

Assign the vocabulary exercise for homework. Have students bring in magazine pictures of people that they think illustrate five adjectives from the exercise. In class, put the pictures around the walls of the room. Have the students walk around and write the adjectives below pictures that they think illustrate them. Explain that more than one answer may be correct, as one person can be described with more than one adjective. For example, a smiling man could be described as *extroverted*, *outgoing*, or *self-assured*. When students are finished, have them explain why they attributed specific adjectives to each person.

Cultural note

Mind your P's and Q's Parents use the idiom *mind your P's and Q's* with their children to mean "be careful and polite," especially in a particular social situation. In the context of the reading, however, the expression is used literally to mean "be careful about how you form your letters."

READING 1 — What do our possessions say about us?
Pages 66-67

This reading describes the results of a study linking possessions to personality.

Additional vocabulary

> **adept:** skilled
> **agreeableness:** the quality of being pleasant
> **erroneously:** wrongly or falsely
> **get some measure of (something):** find out what (something) is like
> **furtively:** secretly and often quickly
> **leak out:** become known
> **morale:** the confidence and desire to succeed felt by a group of people
> **nose through:** look through (somebody's personal or private things)
> **not to be messed with:** not to become involved with (especially because dangerous)
> **rater:** a person who assesses something and ranks it
> **ruthlessly:** in a cruel and uncaring way
> **stifle:** stop from expressing oneself

Reading skill

Recognizing similarity in meaning

See the Teaching suggestions on page 31.

Additional activity

Before students read the text, take items out of your handbag or briefcase and show them to the class. Have a volunteer list the items on the board. Then have students speculate about your life and personality using information from the items in pairs. For example:

1. Our teacher has a picture of two children. They are probably her children. (speculation about fact)

2. Our teacher has a large appointment book. She is probably very organized. (speculation about personality)

Elicit their ideas and tell them if they have guessed correctly.

> **ANSWERS**
> **Reading**
> 1, 4
> **A**
> 1. b   2. d   3. f   4. a   5. e   6. c
> **B**
> 1. I   3. ?   5. I   7. I
> 2. I   4. R   6. R   8. I

41 Unit 9 • Personality

READING 2: The role of temperament in shaping individuality
Pages 68-69

This reading describes how people's temperaments and personalities affect their behavior.

Additional vocabulary

complex: involving a lot of different but related parts
disposition: a person's usual behavior or mood
excitable: easy to excite
full-blown: fully developed
piece together: put parts of something together
rest on: depend on
slow to anger: not get angry very easily
type: identify (someone or something) based on (their sharing) characteristics

Reading skill

Recognizing sources

When you discuss exercise A, ask students to consider what information is in the text. The text does not mention personality disorders, so probably number 2 is incorrect. It also does not mention ways to improve family relationships, so probably number 3 is incorrect. However, it does discuss human behavior, and it includes technical definitions from the field of psychology. Therefore, number 1 is the most likely source.

STRATEGY: Encourage students to eliminate incorrect answers and explain why these choices are not correct.

ANSWERS

Reading
3

A
1

B
1. d   2. c   3. a   4. f   5. b   6. e

C
a. 5   b. 7   c. 2   d. 6   e. 1   f. 4   g. 3

Unit 9 • Personality

READING 3 Mind your P's and Q's
Pages 70-71

This reading presents some information about handwriting analysis.

Additional vocabulary

> **akin:** similar
> **drift:** move slowly
> **joiner:** someone who likes to join clubs, organizations, teams, etc.
> **Mr. (or Ms.) Right:** the man (or woman) who would be the ideal husband (or wife)
> **sweetie:** a way of addressing someone you love

Additional activity

After students complete the reading and the exercises, have them bring in handwriting samples from people they know well (e.g., a close friend or relative). Have the students use the information from the reading to analyze the samples. Then elicit whether they think the analyses are accurate.

Reading skill

Guessing meaning from context

See the Teaching suggestions for this skill on page 2.

> **ANSWERS**
> **Reading**
> A. tied to the past; fearful; a "joiner"; gets bogged down in details; athletic
> B. risk-taker; unafraid of the future; tired, sad, or depressed; needy; insecure; self-centered; immature
> C. optimistic; hard to get close to; independent; grasps the "big picture"; intellectual, thinking type
>
> **After you read**
> **A**
> 1. e   2. d   3. f   4. g   5. b   6. a   7. c
> **B**
> 1. A   2. C   3. A, B   4. A   5. C   6. B

WRAP-UP
Page 72

ANSWERS

Crossword puzzle

Across	Down
1. optimistic	2. intellectual
3. self-centered	4. conscientious
8. withdrawn	5. inhibited
11. boisterous	6. aggressive
12. undependable	7. unconventional
14. outgoing	9. restless
15. sullen	10. self-assured
	13. excitable

Additional activity

For homework, have students write (or, preferably, type) a brief description of their temperament and personality. Make sure they do not put their names on the descriptions and do not include information about their physical appearance. In class, collect the descriptions, shuffle them, and pass them out to different students. Have the students read the descriptions and guess who wrote each one.

UNIT 10 Celebrity

PREVIEW
Page 73

Additional vocabulary

> **fan club:** an organization for people who admire the same music star, football team, etc.
> **hound:** someone who eagerly pursues someone or something
> **icon:** a famous person or thing that represents something important
> **idol:** a person who is greatly loved, admired, or respected
> **in the limelight:** at the center of people's attention
> **offstage:** in private life
> **paparazzi:** the photographers who follow famous people in order to photograph them
> **shudder:** shake, as from cold or fear

Additional activity

Bring in magazine pictures of famous celebrities. Divide the class into two or more teams. Put the pictures up on the walls around the room, and write a number under each one. Have each team write down the names of as many celebrities as they can. The team who identifies the most celebrities correctly wins.

READING 1 — I'm just another kid from Brooklyn
Pages 74–75

This reading describes how movie director Woody Allen feels about being a celebrity.

Additional vocabulary

> **corduroys:** trousers made of thick cotton material with soft raised lines
> **cult:** someone or something that has become very popular with a group of people
> **demonstrative:** expressing emotion openly
> **perk:** an advantage or benefit, such as money or goods, that you get because of your job
> **take it:** accept; receive willingly
> **thriving:** very successful
> **trademark:** typical of (something or someone)

Reading skill

Making restatements

As students complete exercise B, have them find the information in the text that led to their conclusion about whether each statement is a restatement. Then have them write the number of the statement next to the information in the text.

> **ANSWERS**
> **Reading**
> 1. b   2. d   3. a   4. c
> **After you read**
> **A**
> 1. h   3. f   5. g   7. b
> 2. d   4. a   6. e   8. c
> **B**
> 2, 4

Cultural note

Knicks games The *Knicks* are a professional basketball team in New York City. The official name of the team is the New York Knickerbockers, but most people call them the Knicks for short. Woody Allen is an avid basketball fan.

READING 2 California law has paparazzi shuddering
Pages 76-77

This reading describes a law to stop photographers who follow California's celebrities.

Additional vocabulary

> **aim at:** direct something that you do or say or write towards achieving something
> **contend:** state as the truth; claim
> **freelance:** working for different employers rather than for one company
> **personnel:** employees
> **snap a shot:** take a photograph
> **snoop:** try to find out about other people's private lives
> **wording:** exact choice and meaning of words used

Reading skill

Guessing meaning from context

Explain that sometimes unfamiliar words and expressions are followed by examples. For example, the sentences that follow the expression *clamp down* in par. 2 give examples of how the law is clamping down on paparazzi (i.e., by prohibiting trespassing, use of high-tech devices to take pictures on private property, and persistence in following or chasing the celebrity). Point out to students that if they understand just one of the examples, they may be able to figure out that *clamp down* means "control."

STRATEGY: When trying to guess the meaning of an unfamiliar word or expression, look for examples in the sentences that follow it.

ANSWERS

Reading
3

After you read

A
a. 4   c. 5   e. 2
b. 3   d. 6, 7, 8   f. 1

B
1. c   2. e   3. a   4. d   5. b

C
Arguments against the law
1. restricts people from doing their job
2. violates freedom of the press
3. wording is too vague

Arguments in favor of the law
1. celebrities' right to privacy
2. still allows the press to do its job
3. fair because it only punishes the press when it invades privacy

---

READING 3 — Fan club confessions
Pages 78-79

This reading presents results of a study on how celebrities influence the lives of their fans.

Additional vocabulary

bring something in line with (something else): make something more similar to (something else)
cite: mention; refer to
crush: a strong but temporary attraction for someone
mentor: a person who gives help and advice
mold: influence the development of
perennially: constantly; always
pursuit: a hobby or interest
scrapbook: a notebook where people keep memorable pictures, tickets, articles, etc.
starry-eyed: too happy and hopeful, in a way that is not realistic
undertake: do or begin to do something

Additional activity

Bring fashion magazines to class. Divide the class into small groups. Give each group a magazine and have them find examples of "looks" they think were inspired by a celebrity. Specific things to look for include hairstyles, clothing, facial expressions, physical type, makeup, and accessories. Then have the groups hold up the pictures and identify the "look" and celebrity they think inspired it.

Reading skill

Recognizing audience

Before students identify the audience, ask them what kind of information each type of audience might want to read. For example, members of celebrity fan clubs might want to read about a specific celebrity's life, executives in the entertainment industry might be interested in business, psychologists might look at research studies with specialized terminology, and people interested in psychology might be interested in people's behavior. Then have them highlight words related to each of these interests. Since the text contains words such as *behavior* and *self-worth*, the intended audience is probably people who are interested in psychology.

STRATEGY: Encourage students to identify the interests of different audiences and identify words in the text that are related to each interest.

ANSWERS

Reading
1. F (Very few respondents reported altering their physical appearance to appear more similar to their idols.)
2. F (One quarter of the respondents reported changing aspects of their personality to be more like their idol.)
3. T
4. T
5. T
6. F (Women tend to select male idols that they are attracted to.)

After you read

A
4

B
1. To determine whether attachment to celebrity affects people's behavior and feelings about themselves.
2. 200
3. 79

continued on next page

4. a. How much time and money have you spent on your idol?
     b. How much influence do you feel your idol has on you?
     c. How do you feel about yourself?
     d. Have you ever altered your physical appearance to look more like your idol?
     e. Have you ever tried to make your personality more in line with that of your idol?
  5. Attachment to celebrities molds young people's self-identity, but they often don't acknowledge or recognize these effects.

Cultural notes

Brad Pitt *Brad Pitt* is a famous American movie actor. Many people consider him to be very attractive.

Princess Di *Princess Di* is the affectionate nickname for the late Diana, Princess of Wales.

WRAP-UP
Page 80

ANSWERS

A
1. f   3. i   5. g   7. h   9. d
2. a   4. j   6. c   8. e   10. b

B
1. outsmarted   6. outgrew
2. outsell   7. outrun
3. outlive   8. outnumber
4. outplayed   9. outdistances
5. outdo   10. outlast

Additional activity

Have students read an article from a magazine, a newspaper, or the Internet about a favorite celebrity. Then have them prepare a written or oral report for the class.

UNIT 11 The circus

PREVIEW
Page 81

Additional vocabulary

> **acrobat:** an athlete who performs acts requiring skill, agility, and coordination
> **aerialist:** a person who performs difficult and skillful physical actions in the air
> **glimpse:** a brief view
> **pantomime:** a performance using gestures and body movements but no words
> **slapstick:** an energetic type of comedy with chases, collisions, and practical jokes
> **stilt-walking:** walking high above the ground on two long pieces of wood

Additional activity

Here is a technique you can use to help build speaking fluency.

1. Have the students line up in two rows facing each other so that each student has a partner. (If there is an odd number of students, students can take turns being the timekeeper.)

2. Choose one question from the unit preview and read it aloud. Give the students one minute to think about the question. Then have one side of the line respond to the question by talking to the person standing across from them. Tell them that they must speak continuously about the topic for one minute.

3. After one minute, call out "Stop!" Then have the other side of the line respond to the same question.

4. After one minute, call out, "Change!" and have everyone on one side move to the right so that everyone now has a new partner. (The person at the end of the line moves to the beginning of the line).

5. Choose another preview question, and follow steps 1–4. Continue as needed.

> **ANSWERS**
> *Circus performers:* acrobat, aerialist, animal trainer
> *Circus acts:* pantomime, slapstick, stilt-walking

READING 1 Getting serious about clowning

Pages 82-83

This reading explains what makes people want to become circus clowns.

Additional vocabulary

batch: group
be behind (someone) all the way: support (someone) completely
catch the (circus) bug: develop a strong enthusiasm for something
in a heartbeat: immediately
massage therapist: someone who rubs parts of the body to stimulate circulation and promote relaxation
pratfall: a fall in which a performer lands on his or her bottom, especially for an amusing effect
raise a few eyebrows: shock or surprise people
recruiter: a person whose job is to find new employees for companies
sandbox: a box filled with sand where young children can play
traced back to: discovered to originally happen in
wannabe: an ambitious young person who wants a specific role or position

Reading skill

Recognizing similarity in meaning

See the Teaching suggestions for this skill on page 31.

ANSWERS

Reading
3

After you read

A
1. g   3. f   5. d   7. b
2. c   4. h   6. a   8. e

B
1. clown
2. 84
3. two month
4. pratfall
5. pantomime
6. slapstick
7. stilt-walking
8. audition
9. two

Cultural notes

Running off with the circus In the United States and Canada, many people associate the circus with unconventionality and freedom from responsibility. This stereotype is probably due to several factors. First, circus "work" may seem more like play. Second, circus performers lead nomadic lives, never staying in any one place for too long. Third, unconventional people are often drawn to working at the circus. Therefore, children who think they don't have enough freedom may say, "I'm running off with the circus" or "I'm going to run away and join the circus."

Ringling Brothers and Barnum & Bailey Circus *Ringling Brothers and Barnum & Bailey Circus* is one of the largest and most famous circuses in the United States. P. T. Barnum used to promote the circus by referring to it as "the Greatest Show on Earth."

Additional activity

Discuss the stereotype of the circus life and the expression *running off with the circus* from the Cultural Notes. Ask the students if they know of other stereotypes or expressions related to the circus.

READING 2 Circus town
Pages 84-85

This reading provides a glimpse into the lives of circus performers.

Additional vocabulary

> **as ancient lore would have it:** according to traditional stories
> **constancy:** the condition of always staying the same
> **enclave:** enclosed area
> **freak:** in the circus, a very strange or deformed person
> **loser:** a person who is always unsuccessful
> **nomadic:** moving from one place to another
> **preside over:** be in charge of
> **scrutiny:** careful and detailed examination
> **stagehand:** a person whose job is to move the equipment on the stage
> **steeped in:** surrounded by
> **subsidized:** partially paid for
> **upbringing:** training received during childhood

Reading skill

Understanding main ideas

Remind students that it is important to recognize the difference between main ideas and details. Have the students complete exercise B without looking back at the text. Tell them they don't have to remember each paragraph to get most answers correct. Rather, encourage them to determine which of the two statements is more general, expressing an idea, attitude, or opinion rather than just a fact. In most cases, that statement will be the main idea. After they complete the exercise, have them look at the text to check their answers.

STRATEGY: Encourage students to look for sentences in a text that contain not just facts, but ideas, opinions, or attitudes. These sentences usually contain the main ideas.

ANSWERS

Reading
1, 2, 3, 6

After you read

A
1. delirium
2. lore
3. wholesome
4. communal
5. antics
6. squirm
7. bond
8. partition

B
1. b 2. b 3. a 4. a 5. a 6. b

READING 3 — Tragedy at the circus; Circus safe for animals
Pages 86-87

This reading presents opposing views on the issue of using animals in the circus.

Additional vocabulary

> **add up to:** result in
> **be taken aback:** be so surprised that you don't know how to respond
> **bill oneself as:** describe oneself as
> **dwindling:** gradually decreasing in amount or number
> **habitat:** the natural surroundings of a plant or animal
> **heightened:** increased, especially an emotion or effect
> **so-called:** incorrectly or falsely named
> **would-be:** wanting or trying to be

Reading skill

Distinguishing fact from opinion

Learning to distinguish fact from opinion is an important skill. Tell students to think about whether the information can be proven. Teach them to recognize positive or negative words or strongly emotional language, as this may indicate the writer's tone and opinion about a topic. In exercise A, item 1 is a fact because it is possible to prove what the circus officials said. However, in item 2 the words *simply, ignore, ethical issues,* and *left behind* show the writer's negative tone.

STRATEGY: Encourage students to determine whether information in a text can be proven and whether it contains strongly negative, positive, or strongly emotional language.

> **ANSWERS**
>
> **Reading**
> *Answers will vary.*
>
> **After you read**
>
> **A**
> 1. F   2. O   3. F   4. F   5. O   6. O
>
> **B**
> 1. a   2. b   3. c

Cultural note

Animal rights activists In many parts of the world, there are organizations that exist to protect the rights of animals. Such an organization is People for the Ethical Treatment of Animals (PETA). PETA and similar organizations are opposed to the use of animals in circuses, zoos, laboratory experiments, and clothing manufacturing (including furs and leather). They promote vegetarianism and often protest businesses or organizations that use animals in ways PETA considers unethical.

WRAP-UP
Page 88

> **ANSWERS**
>
> **A**
> 1. f   2. j   3. h   4. a   5. e   6. d   7. i   8. g
>
> **B**
> 1. Run away
> 2. passing through
> 3. fork over
> 4. sit back
> 5. try out
> 6. turned away
> 7. look after
> 8. go on

Additional activity

The topic of this reading is suitable for a debate. Divide students into three teams: one in favor of having animals perform in circuses, one against, and one team of judges. See the Teaching suggestion for this activity on page 25.

UNIT 12 Martial arts

PREVIEW
Page 89

Additional vocabulary

> **agility:** the ability to move about quickly and easily
> **cognitive:** connected with thinking or conscious mental processes
> **limb:** an arm or leg of a person or animal
> **routine:** a set of particular movements
> **slash:** use a careless swinging motion
> **slug:** hit
> **swipe:** hit or try to hit (something) especially with a sideways movement
> **thrust:** push forcefully

Additional activity

If possible, bring in a poster or advertisement for a Jackie Chan (or other martial arts) movie. Hold it up and ask if anyone is familiar with this type of movie. Ask if anyone can explain the differences between *karate, kung fu,* and *tae kwon do*. If no one knows, assign different students to research each martial art and report back to the class.

READING 1 Shaolin Temple
Pages 90-91

This reading describes the home of Asian martial arts.

Additional vocabulary

> **acclaimed:** publicly recognized; famous
> **accomplished:** skilled
> **apt to:** likely to
> **artifact:** an object that someone made, especially one of historical interest
> **bizarre:** very strange
> **charge:** accusation
> **enlightenment:** the highest spiritual state that can be reached in Hinduism or Buddhism
> **grounds:** gardens and land around a building
> **kung fu:** a Chinese martial art that involves using your hands and feet as weapons

continued on next page

limber up: prepare the body for active physical exercise
monk: a member of a group of religious men who do not marry and usually live together in a monastery
persevere: continue to do something in a determined way, despite difficulties
staff: a strong stick held in the hand
Zen Buddhism: branch of the Buddhist religion that promotes the practice of meditation

Reading skill

Understanding text organization

Before the students do exercise C, make photocopies of the reading. Cut it into strips so that one paragraph is on each strip of paper. (Make sure the paragraph numbers are not visible.) Have students work in pairs to put the strips into the correct order. When they have finished, check the order as a class. Then ask which paragraphs were the most difficult to find a place for. Point out clues that can help determine text organization, such as pronouns, determiners, similar topics, synonyms, and transitions.

STRATEGY: Encourage students to look for the devices that writers use to make a text cohesive.

ANSWERS

Reading
1, 3, 5

After you read

A
1. c   2. e   3. a   4. f   5. b   6. d

B
1. Martial arts is a physical expression of Zen, the meditation exercises used in pursuit of spiritual enlightenment.
2. They visit the monastery to enjoy the grounds and ancient buildings. They also watch martial arts routines and monks break hard objects with their heads.
3. Their main purpose is to become accomplished in martial arts.
4. According to legend, Bodhidharma meditated there for nine years. His shadow became imprinted on the cave wall.

C
a. 9   b. 11

READING 2 The karate generation
Pages 92-93

This reading explains why karate has become so popular with young Americans.

Additional vocabulary

> **bent:** a natural skill
> **brace:** a support that holds a body part in the correct position
> **bully:** a person who is cruel, especially to people who are smaller and weaker
> **disability:** difficulty performing everyday activities due to a physical or mental condition
> **dyslexia:** an impaired ability to learn to read
> **gymnastics:** physical exercises that develop strength, balance, and agility
> **modicum:** a small amount
> **rec center:** recreation center; a building used for sports and other leisure activities
> **spina bifida:** a physical condition in which some bones in the back are not correctly developed

Reading skill

Guessing meaning from context

See the Teaching suggestions for this skill on page 2.

> **ANSWERS**
> **Reading**
> 1, 2, 4, 5
> **After you read**
> **A**
> a. 4   b. 6   c. 2   d. 3   e. 7   f. 1   g. 5
> **B**
> 1. dyslexia   4. on the social fringe
> 2. founded   5. relegated to the sidelines
> 3. tangible rewards   6. perceived competence

Cultural note

Blue belt In karate, students wear different colored belts depending on their level of mastery. Students who reach the highest level of mastery wear a black belt.

READING 3 Iron and Silk
Pages 94-95

This reading describes how a young man's martial art skills help get him out of trouble.

Additional vocabulary

conceivably: possibly
manila folder: a folder made of strong light brown paper
on (someone's) behalf: to help (someone)
saber: a type of sword
salute: a formal military greeting, by raising the right hand to the side of the head
touch on: briefly mention
waive: not cause (a rule) to be obeyed
warm up: prepare the body for active physical exercise

Reading skill

Making inferences
See the Teaching suggestions for this skill on page 3.

> **ANSWERS**
>
> **Reading**
> *Answers will vary.*
>
> **After you read**
>
> **A**
> 3
>
> **B**
> A young American at the train station wanted to *leave* China with weapons he had *legally* purchased. He was told the only way for him to leave was to *stay in Canton* and return with the proper documentation. A *little while later*, he came back with a policeman from *Canton*. This policeman *suggested that he give* a martial arts demonstration. The *crowd watching the demonstration* finally convinced the officials to let him get on the train *with* the weapons.
>
> **C**
> 1, 4

WRAP-UP
Page 96

ANSWERS

A
1. self-reliance
2. self-pity
3. self-taught
4. self-improvement
5. self-control
6. self-discipline
7. self-portrait
8. self-importance
9. self-interest
10. self-image

B
Positive meaning: self-reliance, self-taught, self-improvement, self-control, self-discipline, self-assured
Negative meaning: self-pity, self-importance, self-interest, self-doubt
Neutral meaning: self-portrait, self-image, self-employed

Additional activity

In pairs, have students choose three or four vocabulary items from the unit to use in a story. Encourage them to use creativity and humor. Ask volunteers to read their stories aloud.

UNIT 13 Fashion

PREVIEW
Page 97

Additional vocabulary

accessory: a clothing item worn or carried for its appearance or usefulness, such as a belt or handbag
attire: clothing
avant-garde: completely new or original
best-dressed: wearing the most stylish clothes
in sync: in harmony
mainstream: most people
out of sync: not in harmony
PDA: personal digital assistant (a small, handheld computer used as a personal organizer)
take off: rise suddenly in success or popularity
trendsetter: a person who starts new trends, especially in fashion

READING 1 Smart clothes
Pages 98-99

This reading describes technological innovations in clothing.

Additional vocabulary

bizarre: strange and unusual
CPU: central processing unit (the electronic system that performs the basic operations of a computer)
data: information
feedback: reaction to a process or activity, or the information obtained from such a reaction
GPS: global positioning system (a system of satellites, computers, and receivers that can calculate where something or someone is)
manual: a small handbook
modem: an electronic device used to connect computers by a telephone line
superimpose: to position (an image) over another image so both can be seen together
vendor: a person or company that sells goods or services
virtual: not real, but created by a computer

Reading skill

Restating

Students sometimes find it difficult to recognize restatements. When students complete this type of exercise, have them underline different modals and modal-like expressions, (e.g., *can, must*) as well as qualifying words (e.g., *currently, probably*) that may slightly change the meaning. Then have them explain how the two statements are similar or different.

Additional activity

In small groups, have students design a set of smart clothes and draw a picture of it. Encourage them to be creative as possible. For example, students could design a coat that adjusts its warmth according to the temperature and makes cups of hot chocolate. Then have the groups present their pictures to the class and explain them.

ANSWERS

Reading
1, 2, 3, 4, 5

After you read

A
1. helps you escape
2. makes it possible
3. don't have to touch
4. at the same time
5. uncomfortable
6. information when you want it

B
1. S   2. S   3. D   4. D

READING 2 — It's a dog's life
Pages 100-101

This reading explores the role of dogs in today's fashion world.

Additional vocabulary

> **aromatherapy:** the use of pleasant smells to improve someone's well-being
> **befitting:** suitable or appropriate for
> **counterpart:** something or someone with the same function or characteristics as another
> **craze:** a fad; something that is very popular for a short time
> **exquisite:** very beautiful or admirable
> **gadget:** a small device with a particular purpose
>
> *continued on next page*

metabolism: the processes in the body that cause food to be used for energy and growth
out of stock: not available for use or sale
sought-after: wanted or desired
sport: wear
take a new turn: get a new meaning
tote bag: a large strong bag

Reading skill

Understanding complex sentences

After students complete the exercise, have them analyze the sentences from the text. First, have them look for the main clause by identifying its subject and verb. Point out that sometimes the verb does not immediately follow its subject. For example, in the answer to item 5, the subject and its verb are separated by a long adjective clause:

A magnetized collar [that is said to increase a dog's circulation, stimulate the
<small>subject</small> <small>adjective clause</small>

appetite and metabolism, and ease stress and fatigue] ***is*** now on sale.
<small>main verb</small>

STRATEGY: Encourage students to identify the main clause when they encounter a complex sentence.

ANSWERS

Reading
All answers are B.

After you read

A
1. ever since fashion models in Japan started revealing their love for their dogs in magazines and on television
2. the brand craze
3. the Hermes' O'Kelly collar
4. a lock similar to the ones found on the brand's famous Kelly handbags
5. a magnetized collar
6. public baths; aromatherapy salons
7. a tiny microphone that hangs around the neck of the animal and a Tamagotchi-like display that can be monitored
8. decorated cakes for special occasions

B
1. Bowlingual
2. sugar-free biscuits or cakes
3. Hermes' O'Kelly collar
4. fragrances
5. a decorated cake
6. a magnetized collar

Cultural notes

Hermes, Burberry, Kate Spade,* and *Gucci *Hermes, Burberry, Kate Spade,* and *Gucci* are the names of famous expensive designer brands.

Tamagotchi *Tamagotchi* is the brand name of a very successful toy from Japan. It's a small electronic device that functions as a "virtual electronic pet." The owner presses buttons on the device to give it virtual food, water, and attention. When the virtual pet "needs" something, the display lights up and emits a sound until the owner responds. If the owner doesn't respond, the pet can "become sick" and even "die" (stop working).

READING 3 — How to separate trends from fads
Pages 102-103

This reading explains why some products and services disappear quickly while others last for years.

Additional vocabulary

> **convert:** change
> **demographics:** characteristics of people in a specific area, especially in relation to their age and spending habits
> **drive (something):** control or push (something)
> **LP:** long-playing record
> **marginal:** very small in amount or effect
> **marketer:** a person who collects and examines information about what people buy
> **premium:** an amount that is more than usual

Reading skill

Guessing meaning from context

See the Teaching suggestions for this skill on page 2.

Additional activity

Discuss question 1 from exercise D as a class. Elicit items that are currently very popular and write them on the board. Then have them use the information from the reading to predict which items are likely to become trends.

ANSWERS

Reading
1. T 3. F 5. T 7. F
2. T 4. F 6. F 8. T

After you read

A
2

B
1. cash in on
2. getting burned
3. takes precedence over
4. accessibility
5. permeating

C
1. N (price)
2. N (ease of adoption, price, availability)
3. A
4. N (appeal, ease of adoption, price)
5. A

WRAP-UP
Page 104

ANSWERS

A
1. CPU   4. BS   7. NASA   10. GED
2. CNN   5. BBC   8. OPEC   11. UNESCO
3. MTV   6. MA   9. LCD   12. PDA

B
Computer terms: CPU, LCD, PDA
Television stations: CNN, MTV, BBC
Organizations: NASA, OPEC, UNESCO
Educational degrees: BS, MA, GED

Additional activity

To review vocabulary items that describe fashion, have the students make their own flash cards. Bring fashion magazines or clothing advertisements, scissors, glue sticks, and index cards to class. Have students cut out pictures that illustrate fashion vocabulary, glue them to cards, and write the vocabulary items on the backs of the cards. Then have them quiz each other in pairs by holding up a picture card and eliciting the correct word. Have pairs change partners when they finish.

UNIT 14 The media

PREVIEW
Page 105

Additional vocabulary

> **air:** broadcast on radio or television
> **cover:** report the details about (an event in the news)
> **curb:** limit; restrict
> **ethics:** standards of what is morally right and wrong
> **flip through:** turn over and read (pages) quickly
> **footage:** film or videotape that shows an event
> **gore:** blood from an injury
> **hypocrite:** a person who pretends to feel or believe something that he or she does not
> **mobilize:** organize (something, such as a group of people) for a purpose
> **outrage:** a feeling of anger and shock
> **tabloid:** a type of newspaper with small pages, many pictures, and short simple reports
> **withhold:** hold back (something)

Additional activity

As the students complete the vocabulary exercise, write the eight statements on the board. When they have finished, ask how many students agree with each statement, and write the results on the board. Ask students why they agree (or don't agree) with each statement.

READING 1 Something strange is happening to tabloids
Pages 106-107

This reading describes how tabloids are trying to establish credibility with the public.

Additional vocabulary

> **alien:** a creature from a different world
> **autopsy:** the cutting open and examination of a dead body to discover the cause of death
> **celeb:** short form of *celebrity*
> **glossy:** produced on shiny paper and usually containing many colored pictures

continued on next page

pal: a friend
sensational: causing intense interest, curiosity, or emotion
slogan: a short, easily remembered phrase used in advertising
spectrum: a range of objects, ideas, or opinions
spicy: slightly shocking (behavior)
splash across: print in a very noticeable way on (something)
UFO: unidentified flying object; an object in the sky that some people think is a ship from another planet
upmarket: designed for high-income consumers

Reading skill

Guessing meaning from context
See the Teaching suggestions for this skill on page 2.

Additional activity

Bring in copies of the tabloids described in the article. Pass them around the class. Have students discuss whether they think the tabloids fit the new, tamer description given in the article.

> **ANSWERS**
> **Reading**
> 1, 2, 3, 7, 8
> **After you read**
> **A**
> 1. halt   3. stand for   5. toned down
> 2. tweak   4. ban   6. tamer
> **B**
> *Possible answers*
> 1. b, e   3. a   5. b, e   7. d, g
> 2. c   4. f   6. g, d

Cultural note

Elvis sightings Since the famous performer Elvis Presley died in 1977, there have been numerous reports that he is not really dead. Periodically, someone claims to have seen Elvis somewhere. This is called an "Elvis sighting." Most people don't believe these claims, and the expression "Elvis sighting" has become synonymous with reports that people think are ridiculous or silly.

READING 2 When our worlds collide
Pages 108-109

This reading explains how journalists choose photos for news magazines.

Additional vocabulary

> **aftermath:** the period following a disaster, the effects of a disaster
> **be after (something or someone):** try to find (something or someone)
> **beat (someone) to (something):** do (something) before (someone else)
> **bring (someone) down:** cause (someone) to lose power or respect
> **coverage:** the reporting of an event in the news
> **dictum:** an authoritative, formal statement
> **exclusive right:** a right to something (e.g., printing or broadcasting a news story) reserved for a specific group
> **guise:** false appearance; disguise
> **keenly:** very strongly
> **sleazy:** dirty, cheap, and not socially acceptable
> **stalk:** follow as closely as possible without being seen or heard
> **when it comes to:** when it is related to

Reading skill

Making inferences

Remind students that an inference is more than just a simple guess. They should always be able to indicate the information in the text on which they based their inference. As students complete exercise B, have them underline the information in the text that led to their inferences.

STRATEGY: Encourage students to underline the information in the text that led to their inferences.

> ## ANSWERS
> **Reading**
> 2
> **After you read**
> **A**
> 1. I justified invading moments of grief under the guise of the reader's right to know.
> 2. Journalists are taught to separate doing the job from worrying about the consequences of publishing what they record.
> 3. We act this way partly because we know that the pictures can have an important meaning.
>
> *continued on next page*

Unit 14 • The media   **67**

> 4. The most keenly sought "exclusives" command tens of thousands of dollars through bidding contests.
> 5. I rarely felt the impact of the story, at least until the coverage was over. . . .
> 6. Now, many people believe journalists are the hypocrites who need to be brought down.
>
> **B**
> 1, 4, 7

Media violence harms children; Media violence does not harm children
Pages 110-111

This reading presents opposing views on the effects of media violence on children and adolescents.

Additional vocabulary

> **circulate:** distribute; pass around
> **collective conscience:** the feelings shared by every member of a group
> **genre:** a style, especially in the arts, that has a particular set of characteristics
> **overwrought:** deeply upset, nervous, and anxious
> **simplemindedness:** a lack of ability to reason or understand
> **throw (something) at (someone):** give (something to someone) in a careless or confusing way

Additional activity

The topic of this reading is suitable for a debate. Divide students into three teams: one that agrees that media violence harms children, one that disagrees, and one team of judges. See the Teaching suggestions for this activity on page 25.

Reading skill

Guessing meaning from context
See the Teaching suggestions for this skill on page 2.

> **ANSWERS**
> **Reading**
> 1. B   2. A   3. A   4. B
> **After you read**
> **A**
> 1. d   2. c   3. f   4. b   5. e   6. a
>
> *continued on next page*

> **B**
> 1. Doctors, therapists, teachers, and youth workers all find themselves struggling to help youngsters. These youngsters are influenced by repeated images of quick, celebratory violence. As a result, they find it increasingly difficult to deal with the inevitable frustrations of daily life.
> 2. We have a lot of trouble understanding complicated issues like the supposed connection between culture and violence. One of the reasons is that so many "experts" are thrown at us. These experts often offer contradictory conclusions.
> 3. Some parents are worried about the impact culture has on their kids. These parents should ignore the headlines and read *The Moral Life of Children*.
>
> **C**
> 1. B
> 3. A

WRAP-UP
Page 112

> **ANSWERS**
>
> **A**
> 1. counterpart
> 2. interpersonal
> 3. misrepresent
> 4. intercontinental
> 5. counterproductive
> 6. counterattack
> 7. misbehave
> 8. misinform
> 9. international
> 10. misunderstand
> 11. interrelated
> 12. counterclockwise
>
> **B**
> 1. interrelated
> 2. counterclockwise
> 3. misunderstood
> 4. misbehave
> 5. counterproductive
> 6. interpersonal
> 7. counterparts
> 8. international
> 9. misrepresent
> 10. misinformed
> 11. intercontinental
> 12. counterattack

Additional activity

Divide the class into two groups. Have one group work together to create an issue of a tabloid. Have the other group work together to create an issue of a newspaper or news magazine. The students can write articles of real events or use their imaginations to create stories.

UNIT 15 Art

PREVIEW
Page 113

Additional vocabulary

corrupt: destroy the honesty or integrity of
curator: a person who manages a museum or library
draw inspiration from: get inspiration from
forgery: a copy of something valuable that is presented as the original
hoard: a secret collection of valuables or money
organic: related to living plants or animals

ANSWERS
1. MT 2. MT 3. MA 4. MT 5. MA 6. MT

Additional activity

After students complete the vocabulary exercise, go over the answers. Ask the students to guess what each article might be about.

READING 1 Girl with a Pitcher
Pages 114-115

This reading reveals how one artist sees and describes the colors he paints.

Additional vocabulary

basin: a bowl-shaped container used for holding food or liquid
bodice: the upper part of a dress
draped: (a cloth) arranged in a particular way
pitcher: a large container used for pouring liquids
turnip: a white root vegetable
ultramarine: bright blue

Reading skill

Recognizing sources

Before students begin the exercise, elicit the type of information that they'd expect to find in each source. When you go over the exercise, point out that the use of the first person (*I*) and the extensive use of dialogue indicate that this excerpt is from a work of fiction.

> **ANSWERS**
> **Reading**
> 1. a, b
> 2. b, c, d, f
> 3. e, j
>
> **After you read**
>
> **A**
> 1
>
> **B**
> 1. D   2. S   3. S   4. S   5. D
>
> **C**
> *Possible answers:*
> 1. She is the painter's servant.
> 2. She is intelligent, observant, curious, sensitive, and uneducated.
> 3. He is demanding, talented, interested in teaching.
> 4. He expects a lot of her and knows that she is intelligent.
> 5. What the artist taught her has changed her perspective. She is now looking at things as an artist.

READING 2 — Organic architecture
Pages 116-117

This reading describes a movement that gets its inspiration from the beauty and harmony of nature.

Additional vocabulary

> **canopy:** a cover or roof for shelter or decoration
> **driftwood:** wood floating in the sea or left on a beach by the action of the waves
> **featured:** displayed
> **fungus:** an organism without leaves or flowers that lives on other plants or decaying matter
> **mollusk:** an animal with a soft body, no backbone, and often a shell
> **prominently:** very noticeably or importantly
> **soaring:** rising very quickly to a high level
> **spire:** a tall pointed structure on top of a building
> **sprawl:** cover a large area of land in a way that looks unplanned
> **stem from:** originate, develop, or grow from
> **strive:** try very hard
> **swirl:** a twisting and circular shape or line
> **wicker:** (made of) very thin pieces of wood that are twisted together

Additional activity

Bring in architecture magazines or pictures of houses in a variety of architectural styles. In small groups, have students discuss which houses they prefer.

Reading skill

Understanding reference words

See the Teaching suggestions for this skill on page 18.

> **ANSWERS**
> **Reading**
> *Answers will vary.*
>
> **After you read**
>
> **A**
> 1. the Rockies
> 2. those forms
> 3. examples of fascinating buildings by 30 contemporary architects from 15 countries
> 4. a desert house
> 5. the sun's heat
> 6. nature
> 7. organic architecture
>
> **B**
> *Picture 1:* a. Renzo Piano b. South Pacific island of New Caledonia c. wicker baskets or curved barrels
> *Picture 2:* a. Kendrick Bangs Kellogg b. Palm Springs, California c. giant fungus or prehistoric bird
> *Picture 3:* a. Bart Prince b. coastal California c. driftwood
> *Picture 4:* a. Douglas Cardinal b. British Columbia c. salmon or mollusk or waves

READING 3 How forgeries corrupt our museums
Pages 118-119

This reading explores whether the works of art in museums are fake or genuine.

Additional vocabulary

> **extent:** amount or degree
> **flourish:** grow or develop successfully
> **looting:** stealing
> **overlap:** how much two things are similar
> **peasant:** member of a low social class of small farmers or farm workers
> **plunder:** steal, especially during a war
> **scale:** size or amount
> **smuggle:** take (something or someone) to or from a place illegally or secretly
> **surface:** appear or become visible

Reading skill

Understanding complex sentences

Point out that looking at punctuation will help students' understanding of complex sentences. For example, a dash (–) often indicates a summary, explanation, or definition. Therefore, in par. 8, the phrase *collectors of antiquities* refers to *private individuals and curators in museums*.

STRATEGY: Encourage students to pay attention to punctuation when trying to understand the meaning of complex sentences.

ANSWERS

Reading

3

After you read

A

1. Peasants didn't really find the silver.
2. Their appearance at that time and place was not an accident.
3. They aren't really ancient.
4. They are not casual discoveries, but planned forgeries.

B

1. allegedly
2. provenance
3. advance the fiction
4. embellished

C

1. a fabulous secret hoard of ancient Middle Eastern silver
2. about 80 percent of the artifacts that pass through the antiquities trade
3. organized gangs of criminals
4. private individuals or curators in museums

WRAP-UP

Page 120

ANSWERS

A

1. egg-shaped
2. star-shaped
3. left-handed
4. blue-eyed
5. long-haired
6. 200-year-old
7. 25-year-old
8. 175-page

continued on next page

B
Possible answers:
1. box-shaped; My house is box-shaped.
2. red-haired; All of his children are red-haired.
3. teary-eyed; I always get teary-eyed when I hear that story.
4. right-handed; I am right-handed, but I eat with my left.
5. 21-year-old; They have a 21-year-old daughter.
6. 300-page; We had to read a 300-page book in one week.

Additional activity

Have students bring pictures of art, antiquities, or architecture they like to class. Have them describe the pieces and explain what they like about them. Encourage them to use vocabulary from the unit.

UNIT 16 Humor

PREVIEW
Page 121

Additional vocabulary

bring down the house: win the audience approval, applause, or laughter
prop: an object that is used in a performance
roll in the aisles: laugh uncontrollably (at a performance)
spontaneity: doing something in a natural, unplanned way
stage presence: confidence and effectiveness achieving a connection with the audience
stand-up comedy: a type of comedy in which the comedian stands in front of the audience and tells jokes

Additional activity

Bring in some cartoons, with the captions removed. Write the captions on the board, and have the students match the captions to the cartoons.

READING 1 So, who's the comedian?
Pages 122-123

This reading describes the experience of a writer who tried to be a stand-up comedian.

Additional vocabulary

bead: a small, usually round piece of material with a hole, often used in necklaces
bit: short theatrical performance that is part of a larger program
debut: a first public appearance
lousy: very bad
orator: a person who gives skillful and effective speeches
pebble: a small, smooth round stone
polish: improve; try to perfect

Additional activity

For homework, have the students think of a joke. Have them tell each other their jokes in small groups. Then have each group choose the best joke and tell it to the class.

Unit 16 • Humor   75

Reading skill

Recognizing tone

See the Teaching suggestions for this skill on page 7.

> **ANSWERS**
>
> **Reading**
> The writer put beads in his mouth and tried to talk. As he put in more and more beads, he began to choke.
>
> **After you read**
> **A**
> 2
>
> **B**
> 1. e 2. d 3. f 4. b 5. g 6. a
>
> **C**
> 1, 3, 5

READING 2 — Taking humor seriously in the workplace
Pages 124-125

This reading explores whether humor has a role in the workplace.

Additional vocabulary

> **burnout:** extreme tiredness, usually caused by working too much
> **choice:** carefully selected
> **cohesion:** the state of unity
> **dissolve:** disappear
> **idleness:** laziness
> **light:** not serious
> **not care one way or the other:** having no feelings for or against (something)
> **perspective:** point of view
> **poke fun at:** laugh at
> **scattered:** disorganized

Reading skill

Restating

See the Teaching suggestions for this skill on page 61.

Unit 16 • Humor

```
ANSWERS
Reading
1. F      2. T      3. F      4. T
After you read
A
2
B
1. c     2. a     3. b     4. e     5. d     6. d
C
1. S     2. D     3. S     4. S     5. D
```

Cultural note

Ziggy Ziggy is a character from a popular comic strip.

READING 3 — Three comedians
Pages 126-127

This reading includes humor samples from three well-known American comedians.

Additional vocabulary

> **afar:** a great distance
> **behold:** look at
> **blow:** destroy; ruin
> **downright:** completely
> **folklore:** unwritten stories of a culture
> **mystical:** beyond ordinary understanding

Additional activity

Students will be more likely to appreciate the humor in the three anecdotes if you read them aloud.

Reading skill | **Making inferences**

See the Teaching suggestions for this skill on page 3.

> **ANSWERS**
>
> **Reading**
> children
>
> **A**
> 1. friends... see your baby
> 2. kids (*or* children) ... I don't know
> 3. wife ... in my house
>
> **B**
> 1. b
> 2. a
> 3. c

WRAP-UP
Page 128

> **ANSWERS**
>
> **A**
> 1. keep a straight face
> 2. burst out laughing; laugh out loud
> 3. be in hysterics; almost die laughing; laugh your head off; roar with laughter
> 4. have someone in stitches; crack people up
>
> **B**
> *Possible answers:*
> 1. laughing their heads off
> 2. cracks me up, has me in stitches
> 3. burst out laughing, almost died laughing, laughed their heads off, roared with laughter
> 4. is in hysterics ... stop themselves from laughing

Additional activity

Have the students draw sketches to illustrate an idiom from the vocabulary expansion. Encourage them to think about the literal meanings of the words in the idioms and use them in their sketches. Draw an example sketch on the board, and have students guess the idiom. Example sketches are:

1. a lion laughing *(roaring with laughter)*
2. a laughing head that is separated from its body *(laugh your head off)*

When all the students have drawn a sketch, have them guess each others' idioms as a class.

Read the text.

1 There are many superstitions associated with weddings. Are they all *nonsense*, or do they have some *merit*? You be the judge.

2 Appropriate wedding attire is an area rich in superstitions. In Puerto Rico, for instance, it is believed that wearing pearls on your wedding day will *doom you to a lifetime of tears*. Wearing diamonds, however, will *ensure brilliant marital success*. In Italy, the groom *wards off* the evil eye by carrying a piece of iron in his pocket. Apparently, the iron *drives away* anyone who might be lurking nearby, ready to place a curse on the *newlyweds*.

3 The *bride and groom* must also be wary of guests *bearing* unlucky gifts. In the Jewish tradition, for example, *accepting* a gift of knives is unlucky. Fortunately, you can neutralize the bad luck by "buying" them for a nominal sum. Apparently, only freebies are unlucky. Since in Chinese the number four is synonymous with death, perhaps the unluckiest gift would be a set of four knives given to a Chinese bride and a Jewish groom.

Complete the exercises.

A Find the words in *italics* in the text. Compare their meanings. Write similar (*S*) or different (*D*). *(50 points)*

_____ 1. *nonsense / merit*

_____ 2. *doom you to a lifetime of tears / ensure brilliant marital success*

_____ 3. *wards off / drives away*

_____ 4. *newlyweds / bride and groom*

_____ 5. *bearing / accepting*

B Check (✔) the statements that are true. *(30 points)*

_____ 1. In Puerto Rico, most brides wear pearls.

_____ 2. If a Jewish couple receives knives as a wedding gift, they may try to pay for them.

_____ 3. It is unlucky for people from different cultures to get married.

C These sentences could be added to the text. Write the sentences that they could follow. *(20 points)*

1. This is because the knives could "cut" the bond between the bride and groom.

_____

2. After all, who wouldn't want a little luck on such an important day?

_____

Name: _____   Date: _____

UNIT 2 QUIZ Read the text.

1 Researchers have reported a *dramatic* rise in obesity among Americans. According to some studies, about 30 percent of American adults are *obese*, and almost 65 percent can be classified as overweight. Many experts agree that obesity is one of the most serious public health challenges of the twenty-first century.

2 The rate of overweight and obese children is especially alarming. An estimated 30 percent of American children are overweight, and about 15 percent of those are obese. The long-term effects of obesity include an increased risk of diabetes, high blood pressure, and heart disease. There are other *adverse* health effects as well.

3 Why are Americans getting so fat? Most experts say the typical American diet is a leading cause of obesity. This diet is comprised of a large percentage of saturated fat, the "bad" fat that makes people vulnerable to heart disease. A lack of physical activity is regarded as another cause of obesity. Most Americans drive rather than walk to school or work. Also, only a fraction of them exercise *on a regular basis*.

Complete the exercises.

A What is the tone of the text? Check (✔) the correct answer. *(10 points)*

_____ 1. sad   _____ 2. serious   _____ 3. angry   _____ 4. critical

B Find the words in *italics* in the reading. Then match each word with its meaning. (Be careful! There is one extra answer.) *(40 points)*

_____ 1. *dramatic*   a. every day

_____ 2. *obese*   b. negative

_____ 3. *adverse*   c. dangerously fat

_____ 4. *on a regular basis* d. surprising and dangerous

                               e. in the same place

C Mark each statement true (*T*) or false (*F*). *(50 points)*

_____ 1. In the United States, a majority of adults weighs more than what is considered normal for their height.

_____ 2. About 70 percent of American children are of normal or less than normal weight for their height.

_____ 3. Obese adults do not have an increased risk of getting diabetes.

_____ 4. Obese children will develop high blood pressure and heart disease as adults.

_____ 5. Only a very small percentage of Americans get enough exercise.

Strategic Reading 3   Copyright © Cambridge University Press

Name: _____ Date: _____

 **Read the text.**

1 Is talent something *innate*, a gift you are born with? Or is it the result of hard work and *perseverance*? Most people think talent in specific areas, such as music or sports, is an innate ability that must be developed through practice. Some researchers, however, question whether innate talent even exists.

2 Those who study child prodigies explain that factors other than innate ability contribute to their early accomplishments. In other words, these so-called geniuses were not born with special skills. Rather, these *precocious* youths were given *ample* early opportunities to develop them. They also spent much more time practicing their skill than their "non-gifted" peers.

3 The fact that certain abilities are rare in one culture but common in others also suggests that talent is learned. For instance, perfect pitch—the ability to hear a musical note and identify the exact *pitch*—is common among speakers of tonal languages such as Chinese or Vietnamese. Among speakers of non-tonal languages, however, it is quite rare. In those cultures, having perfect pitch is seen as a remarkable talent.

Complete the exercises.

A Find the words in *italics* in the text. Circle the meaning of each word. *(40 points)*

1. If you have an *innate* ability to do something, it is **very challenging for you / something you have always been good at / something you have learned to do**.

2. Someone who has *perseverance* **does not give up easily / does not learn easily / does not have a lot of abilities**.

3. If you are given *ample* opportunities to do something, you get **just enough / almost enough / more than enough** chances.

4. A *precocious* child learns to do things **sooner than / later than / worse than** his or her peers.

B Check (✔) the sentences that are true. *(60 points)*

1. _____ A speaker of a tonal language is more likely to be born with perfect pitch than a speaker of a non-tonal language.

2. _____ People who speak tonal languages are more sensitive to pitch because it is an important part of their language.

3. _____ These days, fewer and fewer children are born with talent.

4. _____ Child prodigies usually get more encouragement to practice their skill than other children do.

5. _____ The theory that innate ability does not exist has not yet been proven.

6. _____ Children who have a special talent do not have to work as hard as other children.

Name: _____   Date: _____

UNIT 4 QUIZ Read the text.

1 Is the perception of beauty based on culture? Or is it biological? Many beauty researchers believe that biology *determines* people's ideas about beauty. While they *support* their *ideas* with strong arguments, *undoubtedly* culture still *plays a significant role*.

2 To *back up* their theory, researchers refer to physical attractiveness studies. In these experiments, participants from different cultures looked at photographs of men and women. Even those from very different cultures identified the same features as appealing. This, however, is not *proof* that biology determines people's ideas about physical beauty. Instead, this is more likely *evidence* of a new "universal culture" made possible by the Internet, television, and movies. People in the developed world see images of the same glamorous celebrities and other beautiful people daily. *Certainly*, these images influence their *perceptions* of beauty.

3 It is significant that all of the participants in the studies mentioned above came from developed countries. Participants from developing countries without access to mass media might have responded quite differently.

Complete the exercises.

A Find the words in *italics* in the text. Then match the words that are similar in meaning. *(50 points)*

_____ 1. *determines* (par. 1)   a. *ideas* (par. 1)

_____ 2. *support* (par. 1)   b. *undoubtedly* (par. 1)

_____ 3. *proof* (par. 2)   c. *plays a significant role* (par. 1)

_____ 4. *certainly* (par. 2)   d. *back up* (par. 2)

_____ 5. *perceptions* (par. 2)   e. *evidence* (par. 2)

B What do these words refer to? *(40 points)*

1. *it* (par. 1, line 1)   _____

2. *those* (par. 2, line 3) _____

3. *this* (par. 2, line 4) _____

4. *their* (par. 2, line 8) _____

C Check (✓) the statement that best expresses the writer's point of view. *(10 points)*

_____ 1. The writer does not express an opinion.

_____ 2. The writer believes that biology does not influence human perceptions of beauty.

_____ 3. The writer criticizes the theory that only biology influences human perceptions of beauty.

Name: _____   Date: _____

 **Read the text.**

1 Hit Song Science is a new music analysis system. It compares new songs to a *massive* database of *hit* songs, and predicts their "hit" potential. The system's *promoters* claim that it is adept at recognizing mathematical patterns that make a song appealing to the human ear. According to those who developed the technology, it can do for the record industry what X-rays have done for medicine.

2 Hit Song Science scans a song into its database, and isolates the sound patterns, including *tempo*, melody, and pitch. It then compares them to the sound patterns of hit songs that have been downloaded to its 3-million-song database.

3 Most major music companies currently use the technology because they see it as a way to increase *profitability*. Songwriters, however, *take a different view*. They worry that its use will discourage musicians from taking the creative risks that often lead to the most original forms of artistic expression.

Complete the exercises.

A Find the words in *italics* in the text. Then match each word with its meaning. *(60 points)*

_____ 1. *massive* (par. 1)   a. ability to make money

_____ 2. *hit* (par. 1)   b. rhythm

_____ 3. *promoter* (par. 1)   c. very big

_____ 4. *tempo* (par. 2)   d. very successful

_____ 5. *take a different view* (par. 3)   e. person who supports something

_____ 6. *profitability* (par. 3)   f. disagree

B Mark each statement music company's opinion (*M*) or songwriter's opinion (*S*). *(20 points)*

_____ 1. This technology can save a lot of time and money.

_____ 2. With the use of this technology, songs will all start to sound the same.

C Number the sentences from first step (1) to last step (5). *(20 points)*

_____ a. The computer isolates the song patterns.

_____ b. A new song is scanned into a computer.

_____ c. The computer compares the song patterns to those of hit songs.

_____ d. Record industry executives decide the new song will be a hit.

_____ e. Hit songs are downloaded into a computer's database.

Name: _____   Date: _____

UNIT 6 QUIZ Read the text.

1 Sammy Sosa was suspended from playing professional baseball for using a corked bat, that is, a hollow bat filled with cork. Corked bats are *banned* in professional baseball because they *purportedly* hit balls farther than standard aluminum or wooden bats. At the time of his suspension, Sosa was one of the strongest hitters in the game, with a record of 505 *home runs*.

2 When confronted with the evidence of his transgression, Sosa explained that he normally only used the corked bat during practice to entertain the children who watch him. His use of the bat during an official game was an honest mistake. Before deciding on a penalty, baseball officials examined 76 other bats Sosa used. None of them contained cork.

3 Although baseball officials believed Sosa's explanation, they still gave him a seven-game suspension for using illegal equipment. The public, however, may not be as willing to believe or forgive Sosa. *Only time will tell* whether the ordeal will have a permanent effect on the popular player's reputation.

Complete the exercises.

A Find the words in *italics* in the text. Circle the meaning of each word. *(40 points)*

1. If equipment is *banned* from an official game, players can't **buy / sell / use** it.
2. Something *purportedly* true is **certainly / believed to be / probably not** true.
3. If Sosa hits a *home run*, his team will **win points / lose points / get a penalty**.
4. *Only time will tell* means **things will get better later / we don't know now / we don't know the correct time**.

B Number the events from first event (1) to last event (8). *(50 points)*

_____ a. Sosa used a corked bat during practice.

_____ b. Officials discovered Sosa had used a corked bat.

_____ c. Sosa hit 505 home runs.

_____ d. Sosa explained that he had used the corked bat by mistake.

_____ e. Officials examined Sosa's other bats.

_____ f. Sosa received a seven-game suspension.

_____ g. Sosa used a corked bat during an official game.

_____ h. Officials believed Sosa's explanation.

C Answer the question. *(10 points)*

1. Why do you think children found it entertaining to watch Sosa practice with a corked bat?

_____

Name: _____   Date: _____

 **Read the text.**

1 When an elderly person dies, those left behind are advised to take comfort in the fact that the deceased had a long life. However, in my mind, such platitudes do nothing to ease the pain of losing a loved one.

2 I was 10 years old when my great-grandmother Sadie passed away. At 89, she still had an insatiable appetite for life. I don't ever remember thinking of her as "old," which probably explains why I called her by her given name. Photographs taken just before her death show a stylishly-dressed woman who easily passed for 65.

3 Sadie's death one bright summer morning was met with the shock that usually accompanies the death of a far younger person. At her funeral, hundreds of mourners lined up to offer condolences to our grieving family. When I saw my great-grandmother lying in a coffin, I panicked, convinced that she was still breathing. The last thing I remember is being held tightly in my uncle's arms, watching the hearse take my beloved Sadie to her grave.

Complete the exercises.

A Find the words in the text that match these definitions. Write one word on each line. *(60 points)*

1. _____ _____ _____ : the friends and relatives of someone who has died (par. 1)

2. _____ : meaningless statements (par. 1)

3. _____ _____ _____ : make (someone) feel better (par. 1)

4. _____ _____ : died (par. 2)

5. _____ _____ : great energy and enthusiasm (par. 2)

6. _____ _____ : appeared to be (par. 2)

B Mark each statement true (*T*) or false (*F*). *(40 points)*

_____ 1. The writer was comforted by the fact Sadie lived to be almost 90.

_____ 2. The last photograph of Sadie was taken when she was 65 years old.

_____ 3. The name *Sadie* means "great-grandmother."

_____ 4. The writer rode in the hearse with her great-grandmother's body.

Name: _____ Date: _____

 **Read the text.**

1 Alzheimer's disease affects an estimated 10 percent of people over 65 and nearly 50 percent of those over 85. One of the first signs of Alzheimer's disease is memory loss. It is normal for memory to diminish with age, but Alzheimer's involves more than just simple memory lapses.

2 One sign of Alzheimer's disease is the inability to retain recently learned information. We all forget names or telephone numbers from time to time, but are usually able to recall them *eventually*. People with Alzheimer's not only are much more likely to forget things, but also completely unable to retrieve them later.

3 Another *telltale sign* of Alzheimer's is forgetting how to perform *unconscious tasks* such as opening a door with a key. While many of us might forget to take the keys when we leave the house, a person with Alzheimer's may have no idea what to do with their house key. And although we all misplace things, people with Alzheimer's misplace things in unusual places, such as a shoe in the freezer.

Complete the exercises.

A Find the words in *italics* in the text. Circle the meaning of each word or phrase. *(30 points)*

1. *eventually* (par. 2)
   a. normally
   b. finally

2. *telltale sign* (par. 3)
   a. important indication
   b. significant problem

3. *unconscious tasks* (par. 3)
   a. activities we do almost every day
   b. activities we do without thinking

B Identify which sentence in each pair is the main idea and which is the supporting idea. Write main idea (*M*) or supporting idea (*S*). *(60 points)*

1. _____ a. People without Alzheimer's disease can usually remember information they have just learned.
   _____ b. People with Alzheimer's disease may have trouble remembering names or telephone numbers.

2. _____ a. People with Alzheimer's disease forget how to do simple things.
   _____ b. People without Alzheimer's disease generally remember how to use a key.

3. _____ a. Someone with Alzheimer's disease might put a shoe in the freezer.
   _____ b. People with Alzheimer's disease misplace things in unusual places.

C Check (✔) the main audience for this text. *(10 points)*

_____ 1. doctors who treat Alzheimer's disease

_____ 2. people who are worried about memory loss

Name: _____ Date: _____

UNIT 9 QUIZ Read the text.

1 Do you lack self-assurance in social situations? Are you shy and withdrawn while your brother is a boisterous extrovert? Research suggests that a tendency toward shyness might be *innate*.

2 In an attempt to determine whether shyness can be attributed to inherent differences, scientists conducted a 20-year study. In the first *phase* of the study, a group of two-year-olds were divided into two groups—inhibited and outgoing—based on their behavior. Twenty years later, the same children, now adults, were shown a series of pictures of people with *neutral facial expressions*. After they had become accustomed to the faces, the researchers introduced new faces, also without expression, and measured the subjects' brain activity. When looking at an unfamiliar face, the *subjects* in the shy group showed much more activity in the amygdala, the part of the brain known to control fear.

3 Interestingly, this increased brain activity *showed up* in all of the adults who had been shy as children, despite the fact that many of them no longer suffered from shyness.

Complete the exercises.

A Find the words in *italics* in the text. Circle the meaning of each word. *(50 points)*

1. If a personality trait is *innate*, it is something you **are born with / learn / acquire as an adult**.
2. If a study has different *phases*, it consists of two or more **research questions / steps / groups of participants**.
3. A *neutral facial expression* is **angry / unfamiliar / without emotion**.
4. The *subjects* of a study are its **topics / participants / researchers**.
5. When activity *shows up* on a brain scan, it **is important / appears / disappears**.

B Mark each sentence true (*T*) or false (*F*). *(50 points)*

_____ 1. A tendency toward shyness can be overcome.

_____ 2. Researchers measured the brain activity of two-year-old children.

_____ 3. The adults who participated in the study were 20 years old.

_____ 4. The amygdala is a part of the brain that only shy people have.

_____ 5. Only some participants showed increased brain activity when they saw unfamiliar faces.

Strategic Reading 3   Copyright © Cambridge University Press

Name: _____   Date: _____

 **Read the text.**

1 In the age of mass media, political *figures* are beginning to behave more like celebrities than serious leaders. Many people consider John F. Kennedy Jr., President of the United States from 1960 to 1963, the first "celebrity politician." With his striking good looks, President Kennedy could easily have been *mistaken for* a movie star. However, unlike movie stars who were expected to live in the public eye, in those early days of television politicians were allowed a degree of privacy that would be unimaginable today.

2 While it might seem that forcing politicians to live their lives in the limelight would make them behave more honestly, in fact the opposite is true. Successful politicians have become *adept* actors, expert at giving *vague non-answers* to reporters' questions. Those who answer honestly are singled out and rarely survive the close media attention. Another downside to "political celebrity" is that fewer talented people are willing to become politicians. After all, how many of us would want the press peeking into every corner of our private lives?

Complete the exercises.

A Find the words in *italics* in the text. Then match each word with its meaning. (Be careful! There are two extra answers.) *(40 points)*

_____ 1. *figures* (par. 1)   a. extremely skilled

_____ 2. *mistaken for* (par. 1)   b. challenging questions

_____ 3. *adept* (par. 2)   c. identified incorrectly as

_____ 4. *vague non-answers* (par. 2) d. unsatisfactory responses

                                     e. people

                                     f. made an error about

B Check (✔) the statements that the writer of the text would agree with. *(60 points)*

_____ 1. John F. Kennedy Jr. looked like a movie star.

_____ 2. In the early 1960s, politicians were not given very much privacy.

_____ 3. In the early 1960s, the public was very interested in the lives of celebrities.

_____ 4. Politicians are less likely to behave honestly now than they were in the past.

_____ 5. Intense media attention discourages talented people from becoming politicians.

_____ 6. Politicians who give honest answers do not have very long political careers.

Strategic Reading 3   Copyright © Cambridge University Press

Name: _____   Date: _____

 **Read the text.**

1 Cirque du Soleil, French for "Circus of the Sun," began in 1984 with a simple dream. A group of Canadian street performers known as "Le Club des Talons Hauts" (the high-heels club) got together to entertain audiences, see the world, and have a blast.

2 Unlike traditional circuses, the Cirque du Soleil has no animal performers – just humans. Also, the acts are performed to live, original music. Finally, the Cirque du Soleil has a unique mission. The members, who come from all over the world and all walks of life, are committed to increasing their audience's understanding of and respect for human individuality. At the same time, they are interested in exploring the profound human connections that the multicultural, multigenerational performers share with each other and their audience. Their goal is not only to entertain, but also to enlighten.

3 The performers include acrobats, aerialists, mimes, stilt-walkers, and clowns from over 40 countries, speaking more than 25 languages. Since its founding in 1984, Cirque du Soleil has passed through almost 100 cities, delighting millions of people worldwide.

Complete the exercises.

A Find the words in the text that match these definitions. Write one word on each line. *(50 points)*

1. ___ ___ ___ : jobs or social backgrounds (par. 2)

2. _____ : very deep and important (par. 2)

3. _____ : of all different ages (par. 2)

4. _____ : provide with information and understanding (par. 2)

5. _____ : beginning (par. 3)

B Check (✓) the statement that best expresses the writer's point of view. *(10 points)*

_____ 1. The writer is a fan of the Cirque du Soleil.

_____ 2. The writer thinks animals should not be used in circus acts.

C Check (✓) the statements that are true. *(40 points)*

_____ 1. Traditional circuses usually play recorded music.

_____ 2. The Cirque du Soleil is more interested in providing entertainment than in promoting human understanding.

_____ 3. The Cirque du Soleil has become popular all over the world.

_____ 4. An important part of the Cirque du Soleil's mission is to bring people together.

Name: _____ Date: _____

 **Read the text.**

1 Tae kwon do is one of the martial arts. Translated literally, *tae* means "jump or fly and kick or smash with the foot," *kwon* means "punch or destroy with the fist," and *do* means "the art or way of." Put more simply, tae kwon do can be described as a method of self-defense using the hands and feet. Although the practice of tae kwon do builds one's physical strength and agility, it was actually created as a *means* to discourage violence. Thus, tae kwon do does not involve the use of *offensive* force.

2 According to serious, lifelong *practitioners*, tae kwon do is much more than merely a way to defend oneself physically. Rather, it is an art, a philosophy, and a way of life, the *ultimate* goal of which is a more peaceful world. Through the development of character traits such as self-control, self-reliance, and self-discipline, as well as modeling positive moral and ethical behavior, practitioners believe that individuals can serve as *catalysts* for peace within their families, communities, and nations.

Complete the exercises.

A Find the words in *italics* in the text. Then match each word with its meaning. (Be careful! There is one extra answer.) *(50 points)*

1. _____ *means* (par. 1)   a. people who do something that requires skill
2. _____ *offensive* (par. 1)   b. final and most important
3. _____ *practitioners* (par. 2)   c. way or method
4. _____ *ultimate* (par. 2)   d. extremely bad
5. _____ *catalysts* (par. 2)   e. used for attacking
                                      f. people who cause changes

B Answer the questions. *(30 points)*

1. How do practitioners of tae kwon do feel about violence?

   _____

2. What is the ultimate goal of tae kwon do?

   _____

3. How do practitioners of tae kwon do try to achieve this goal?

   _____

C Which sentences in the text could these sentences follow? Write the sentences. *(20 points)*

1. It originated in Korea, but it is now practiced all over the world.

   _____

2. The theory is that physical strength should be used to prevent violence.

   _____

Strategic Reading 3   Copyright © Cambridge University Press

Name: _____   Date: _____

 **Read the text.**

1 In *The Tipping Point*, author Malcolm Gladwell presents an intriguing theory to explain how trends spread throughout a population. Gladwell argues that any social "epidemic," including a fashion trend, involves a very small group of exceptional people. Gladwell calls this "the law of the few."

2 The law of the few is based on the belief that a very limited number of individuals in any community have vastly more social connections than most of their peers. The endorsement of a fashion trend by one of these individuals almost guarantees that it will permeate their communities.

3 Gladwell calls these trendsetters *connectors* – people with a gift for bringing the world together. According to Gladwell, connectors are typically gregarious, with great personal charisma and energy. Most important, however, is the fact that they have a social circle four times the size of that of their peers. Thus, when connectors endorse a trendy new restaurant, it is likely to become a hit.

Complete the exercises.

A Find the words in the text that match these definitions. Write one word on each line. *(50 points)*

1. _____ : very interesting (par. 1)
2. _____ : something that affects many people (par. 1)
3. _____ : significantly (par. 2)
4. _____ : public statement of approval or support (par. 2)
5. _____ : enjoying the company of other people (par. 3)

B Compare the meaning of each pair of sentences. Write same (*S*) or different (*D*). *(30 points)*

_____ 1. The law is based on the belief that a limited number of individuals have more social connections than most of their peers.

Very few people have more social connections than their peers.

_____ 2. The endorsement of a fashion trend by a connector almost guarantees that it will permeate their communities.

Fashion trends endorsed by connectors usually become popular.

_____ 3. When connectors endorse a trendy new restaurant, it is likely to become a hit.

Restaurants that connectors have endorsed will be very successful.

C Answer the questions. *(20 points)*

1. How are connectors different from other people?

_____

2. Why are connectors better at setting trends?

_____

Strategic Reading 3   Copyright © Cambridge University Press

Name: _____   Date: _____

 **Read the text.**

1 A new type of television show has *taken the public by storm* – reality TV. There are many different types of reality TV shows, but they all share two characteristics. First, the people you see on your screen are not professional actors. Second, although the film or video footage is carefully edited or even tweaked before it is aired, the shows are *largely* unscripted.

2 These reality TV shows are enormously popular with the public, much to the delight of the television industry. Although opinions differ on why the public is so *engrossed* in watching ordinary people misbehaving, doing extraordinarily stupid things, or simply interrelating, there is no disagreement about why the television industry is so enamored of the trend. Compared to *prevailing* television shows, reality TV is cheap to produce. You don't need to hire actors, as most people are eager for the publicity and willing to participate in the shows without pay. Nor is it necessary to hire scriptwriters, or pay for fancy costumes and sets. For television executives, reality TV is a dream come true.

Complete the exercises.

A Find the words in *italics* in the text. Then match each word with its meaning. *(40 points)*

1. _____ *taken the public by storm* (par. 1)   a. standard

2. _____ *largely* (par. 1)   b. suddenly become popular

3. _____ *engrossed* (par. 2)   c. fascinated

4. _____ *prevailing* (par. 2)   d. mostly

B Underline the sentences in the text with the same meaning as the statements below. Write the number of each statement next to the sentence you underline. *(30 points)*

1. Reality television shows do not have a written script, but they are edited.

2. People who work in television are glad that reality TV shows are so popular.

3. There are many theories on the reasons for reality TV's popularity with the public, but only one theory for its popularity with the television industry.

C Answer the questions. *(30 points)*

1. Why are fancy costumes, sets, and scriptwriters unnecessary for reality TV shows?

_____

2. What kinds of things do people do on reality TV shows?

_____

3. Why do you think reality TV shows are "tweaked" before they are aired?

_____

Name: _____   Date: _____

 **Read the text.**

1 David Hockney is a painter. He is also a writer, and with his book, *Secret Knowledge: Rediscovering the Lost Techniques of the Old Masters*, Hockney *ventures* into the world of art history. Hockney's text introduces a theory that has shaken up art curators and historians. Based on a close examination of the canvases of some of the most respected European *masters*, Hockney *sets out* to prove that painters such as Johannes Vermeer, Jan van Eyck and Caravaggio used optical *devices* to aid them in their work.

2 As one piece of evidence for his theory, Hockney points to the remarkably accurate representation of *ornately embellished* fabrics in early Baroque paintings. He *argues* that without using optical *tools*, even *artistic geniuses* would not have been able to paint the *elaborate* patterns with near-photographic accuracy. Without a camera, how did the artists of antiquity do it? Hockney *alleges* that they used lenses, prisms, and mirrors to project images of their subject onto a blank wall. They could then trace the image, ultimately transferring it onto a canvas.

Complete the exercises.

A Match each word with a word that is similar in meaning. *(50 points)*

_____ 1. *ventures* (par. 1)   a. *artistic geniuses* (par. 2)

_____ 2. *masters* (par. 1)   b. *elaborate* (par. 2)

_____ 3. *devices* (par. 1)   c. *sets out* (par. 1)

_____ 4. *ornately embellished* (par. 2)   d. *alleges* (par. 2)

_____ 5. *argues* (par. 2)   e. *tools* (par. 2)

B What do these words refer to? *(20 points)*

1. *them* (par. 1, line 6) _____

2. *it* (par. 2, line 5) _____

C Put these events in order. Number the sentences from first step (1) to last step (6). *(30 points)*

_____ a. The artist places a very thin piece of paper over the reflected image of the subject.

_____ b. The artist sets up the optical device.

_____ c. The artist traces the subject's image onto the thin paper.

_____ d. The artist copies the traced image onto the canvas.

_____ e. The artist fills in the colors and textures with paint.

_____ f. The artist uses the optical device to reflect the subject's image onto a wall.

Strategic Reading 3   Copyright © Cambridge University Press   93

Name: _____   Date: _____

 **Read the text.**

1 In English, there is a saying that "Laughter is the best medicine." Increasingly, science is proving that laughter is an *irreplaceable* part of the body's toolbox.

2 When we burst out laughing, our brains are flooded with chemicals known as endorphins. Endorphins act as natural *painkillers* and play a critical role in the *regulation* of mood. Another benefit of laughing is that we take in a lot of oxygen. Increased levels of oxygen in the bloodstream have been proven to *augment* energy, providing relief from both fatigue and depression.

3 Sometimes, when an especially good joke cracks us up, we laugh so hard that we cry. Crying has several benefits. First, tears wash harmful dirt out of our eyes. Second, if we are in hysterics for long enough, our noses will start running and wash away *irritants* from the *sinuses*. Finally, both laughing and crying allow us to release tension, *simultaneously* exercising and relaxing many of the body's muscles.

Complete the exercises.

A Find the words in *italics* in the text. Then match each word to its meaning. *(70 points)*

_____ 1. *irreplaceable* (par. 1)   a. improve

_____ 2. *regulation* (par. 2)   b. at the same time

_____ 3. *augment* (par. 2)   c. unique and extremely important

_____ 4. *irritants* (par. 3)   d. something that stops pain

_____ 5. *sinuses* (par. 3)   e. things that bother you

_____ 6. *simultaneously* (par. 3)   f. control

_____ 7. *painkillers* (par. 2)   g. a part of the nose and throat

B Circle the answer that is *not* mentioned in the reading. *(30 points)*

1. What happens in the body when we laugh?

    a. More oxygen enters our blood and brain.

    b. Our muscles tighten and relax.

    c. Our heart rate decreases.

2. What functions do endorphins have in the brain?

    a. They reduce pain.

    b. They help us think more clearly.

    c. They make us feel happier.

3. What are the benefits of crying?

    a. It makes it easier to breathe.

    b. It cleans out our eyes.

    c. It makes us feel less stressed.

Unit quiz answers

UNIT 1 QUIZ

A
1. D 2. D 3. S 4. S 5. D

B
3

C
1. In the Jewish tradition, for example, accepting a gift of knives is unlucky.
2. There are many superstitions associated with weddings.

UNIT 2 QUIZ

A
2

B
1. d 2. c 3. b 4. a

C
1. T 2. T 3. F 4. F 5. T

UNIT 3 QUIZ

A
1. something you have always been good at
2. does not give up easily
3. more than enough
4. sooner than

B
2, 4, 5

UNIT 4 QUIZ

A
1. c 2. d 3. e 4. b 5. a

B
1. the perception of beauty
2. participants
3. identifying the same features as appealing
4. people in the developed world

C
3

UNIT 5 QUIZ

A
1. c 2. d 3. e 4. b 5. f 6. a

B
1. M 2. M 3. S 4. M

C
a. 2 b. 5 c. 1 d. 3 e. 4

UNIT 6 QUIZ

A
1. use
2. believed to be
3. win points
4. we don't know right now

B
a. 2 c. 1 e. 6 g. 3
b. 4 d. 5 f. 8 h. 7

C
Possible answers:
1. He could hit the ball farther. (*Or:* He could hit more home runs.)

UNIT 7 QUIZ

A
1. those left behind   4. passed away
2. platitudes   5. insatiable appetite
3. ease the pain   6. passed for

B
1. F 2. F 3. F 4. F

UNIT 8 QUIZ

A
1. b 2. a 3. b

B
1. a. M b. S   2. a. M b. S   3. a. S b. M

C
2

UNIT 9 QUIZ

A
1. are born with
2. steps
3. without expression
4. participants
5. appears

B
1. T 2. F 3. F 4. F 5. T

UNIT 10 QUIZ

A
1. e 2. c 3. a 4. d

B
1, 3, 4, 5, 6

UNIT 11 QUIZ

A
1. walks of life
2. profound
3. multi-generational
4. enlighten
5. founding

B
1

C
1, 3, 4

UNIT 12 QUIZ

A
1. c 2. e 3. a 4. b 5. f

B
Possible answers:
1. They discourage it and only use it to defend themselves.
2. They try to develop positive character traits, such as ethics and morality.
3. The ultimate goal is a more peaceful world.

C
1. Tae kwon do is one of the martial arts.
2. Although the practice of tae kwon do builds one's physical strength and agility, it was actually created as a *means* to discourage violence.

UNIT 13 QUIZ

A
1. intriguing
2. epidemic
3. vastly
4. endorsement
5. gregarious

B
1. D 2. S 3. S

C
Possible answers:
1. They have many more social contacts, and they are charismatic, energetic, and gregarious.
2. They spread the word about a trend to their large social circle quickly and effectively.

UNIT 14 QUIZ

A
1. b 2. d 3. c 4. a

B
1. Second, although the film or video footage . . . largely unscripted. (par. 1, lines 3–5)
2. These reality T.V. shows . . . of the television industry. (par. 2, lines 1–2)
3. Although opinions differ . . . of the trend. (par. 2, lines 2–5)

C
Possible answers:
1. The shows involve ordinary people.
2. They misbehave, do stupid things, and just interrelate with each other.
3. A lot of video or film footage is inappropriate or boring.

UNIT 15 QUIZ

A
1. c 2. a 3. e 4. b 5. d

B
1. painters such as Vermeer, van Eyck, and Caravaggio
2. paint with near-photographic accuracy

C
a. 3 b. 1 c. 4 d. 5 e. 6 f. 2

UNIT 16 QUIZ

A
1. c 2. f 3. a 4. e 5. g 6. b
7. d

B
1. c 2. b 3. a